pre**fab** elements

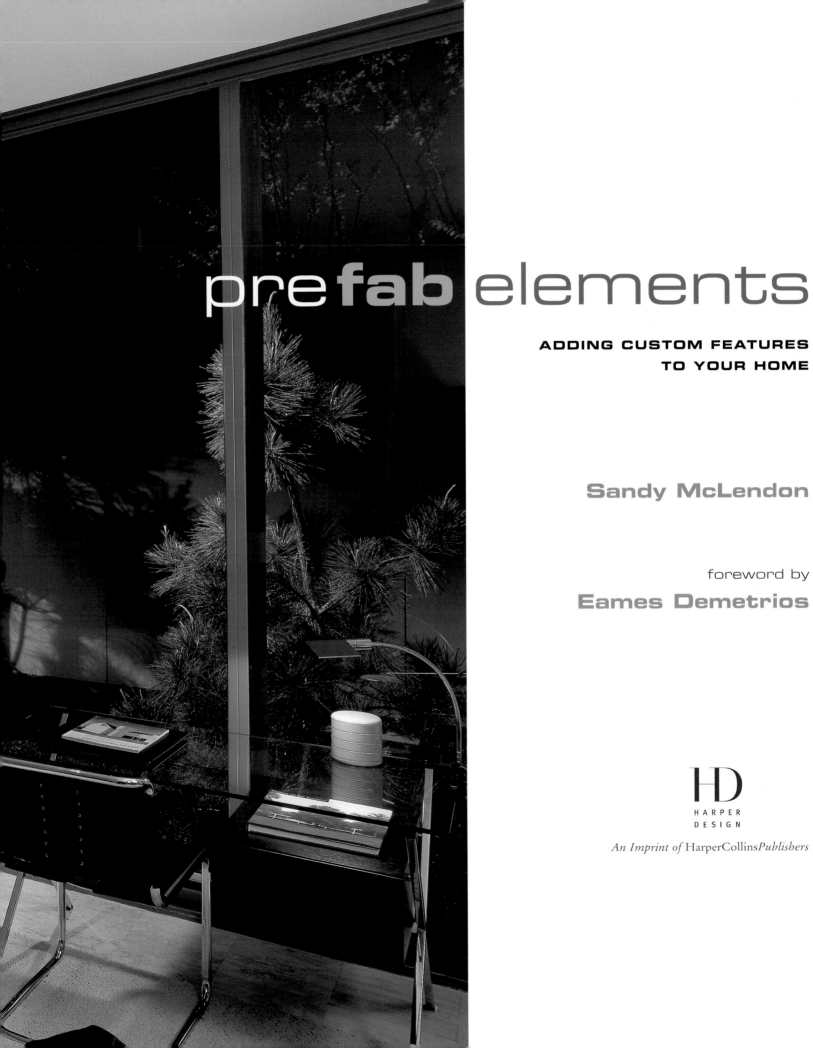

prefab elements

ADDING CUSTOM FEATURES
TO YOUR HOME

Sandy McLendon

foreword by
Eames Demetrios

HARPER
DESIGN

An Imprint of HarperCollins*Publishers*

PREFAB ELEMENTS: Adding Custom Features to Your Home

Copyright © 2005 by GLITTERATI INCORPORATED
www.GlitteratiIncorporated.com

Text copyright © 2005 by Sandy McLendon
Foreword copyright © 2005 by Eames Demetrios

First published in 2005 by:
Harper Design
An Imprint of HarperCollins*Publishers*
10 East 53rd Street
New York, NY 10022
Tel: (212) 207-7000
Fax: (212) 207-7654
HarperDesign@harpercollins.com
www.harpercollins.com

Distributed throughout the world by:
HarperCollins International
10 East 53rd Street
New York, NY 10022
Fax: (212) 207-7654

HarperCollins books may be purchased for educational, business, or sales
promotional use. For information, please write: Special Markets Department,
HarperCollins *Publishers* Inc., 10 East 53rd Street, New York, NY 10022.

Design: Susi Oberhelman

Library of Congress Cataloging-in-Publication Data

McLendon, Sandy.
    Prefab elements : adding custom features to your home /
by Sandy McLendon.
        p. cm.
    Includes index.
    ISBN 0-06-075162-2 (hardcover)
    1. Prefabricated houses–Remodeling.   I. Title.
    TH4819.P7M35 2005
    643'.7–dc22

                          2005007097

FIRST EDITION

Printed and bound in China

1 2 3 4 5 6 7 / 11 10 09 08 07 06 05

FIRST PRINTING, 2005

Redi-Rock prefab patio system.

contents

	Foreword	8
	By Eames Demetrios	
	Introduction	12
	Building Blocks for the House You Want	
CHAPTER 1	**History and Promise**	14
	Prefab Then and Now	16
CHAPTER 2	**Putting It Together**	50
	A Selection of Prefab Elements	52
	Foundations & Floor Structures	54
	Walls	62
	Glazing	74
	Interior Elements	82
	Roofs	98
	Prefab Room Additions	102
CHAPTER 3	**Using Prefab Elements**	114
	Homes on the Cutting Edge	116
CHAPTER 4	**Computer-Assisted Design**	122
	Tools You Can Use	124
	Glossary	128
	Sources	133
	Credits	138
	Index	141

Oskar Leo Kaufman's OA.SYS system interior.

foreword

by E A M E S   D E M E T R I O S

Each week seems to bring news of yet another cool-looking modern prefab house. Many are beautiful but none have really yet achieved their implicit goal: to be inhabited in quantity. But I believe that may be about to change—and that change will mark the next generation of prefab. Until now—and continuing as I write—prefabrication has concealed modernism (or more accurately concealed its own process) rather than embrace it. In spite of this, many of this generation's most intriguing architects are exploring mass-produced housing. On the consumer side, a perfect storm of real estate values (with all their attendant opportunities and costs), growing awareness of design, sustainability, and plain old economic pressure have created a real hunger for the right affordable solution.

If you imagine yourself holding an updated edition of this book in four or five years, we'll all know by then if prefabrication rose to the challenge at this tantalizing potential moment. Most of us believe the holy grail is out there: the mass produced house that celebrates and draws aesthetic, functional, and sustainable richness from its prefabrication, while still providing a good living to those who put it together. One can easily draw a distinction between that dream and those disheveled and bisected tract houses that periodically bloat down our freeways in slow-witted pairs, attended by flashing Wide Load chaperones and that lack even the satisfaction of a well-done trailer when assembled.

What the greater community needs is houses at that Wide Load price point but that have taken up the gauntlet of modern industrial design at its best. The architect of the successful prefab house will have something in common with the writer of good popular music: Top 10 status is not merely a sign of economic success, it is a symbol of having connected to millions of other people. And sure, a few hacks will slip in there, but in the best eras, the tension the Lennon/McCartneys or the Holland/Dozier/Hollands feel between a pure vision and the desire for connection leads to beautiful pop music.

Few would disagree that there is more to be done with prefabricated housing, particularly in the modern idiom, but can there possibly be a need for another book—at least until this next generation of prefabricated homes truly enters the world?

Perhaps, this book, if you look at the details rather than the whole, is a legacy of the last modernist prefab moment—the Case Study House program (1945–66). When the Eames House (Case Study House #8) was built in 1949 by my grandparents, architects Charles and Ray Eames, the available parts came largely from factories. They drew from a whole shelf of catalogues—including at least one with parts intended for ocean cruise liners. Today, as this book dissects for the reader, the battle for the set pieces of home construction has been largely won by prefabrication but it has not yet become, on the whole, a refined aesthetic.

This is part of the challenge of the upcoming generation of prefabricated homes. In other areas of industrial design, excellence and mass production go hand in hand. This is not yet the case with most prefabricated homes available today. However, in this book, we

Eames House (Case Study House #8) exterior.

see the seeds of how this might be achieved in the future. And beyond what we see here, in the next 20 years, green issues are going to be mainstream—clients will consider it as normal to weigh sustainability as they do now to factor in price, square footage, or snow load. In a way it may be very much like snow load or seismic concerns, customized to the norms of each locale. Prefab houses and prefab parts would seem to lend themselves to these issues, because it would allow the modern consumer to make environmentally friendly choices about sophisticated systems that mesh with their lifestyle.

And that is what all these houses, no more or less prefab than their custom brethren must provide: a place to live. Simple but hard. Difficult, but doable. When my brothers and sisters and I visited our grandparents' house and played in the room you see on the facing page, that's all it was to us: our grandparents' house. It was not a kit-of-parts. Not an icon of modernism. Not prefab. It wasn't even the famous Eames House or Case Study House #8. It was just a great place to visit. It was a lot of fun.

As we have grown up, we love and respect that house more and more, but we do so precisely because Charles and Ray did all the things on that list but never at the expense of it being a home. The Eames House is famous for all sorts of reasons, thousands of visitors still make an appointment each year to see it and its beautiful grounds, but none of that would have mattered if it hadn't been a home as well as a building. Case Study House #8 let its inhabitants live their life the best way they could. Should any prefab home do less? ■

Eames House (Case Study House #8) interior.

introduction

We're all trying to find the house of our dream—and like so many of our dreams, our housing is almost never quite what we see in our reveries. We have budgets, lender requirements, building codes, and conflicting needs from different family members to contend with. All these things, and more, compromise our houses; we almost never achieve what we can conceive.

Owning a house at all is a fairly remarkable accomplishment today; the median price of an American house is now $170,000, and in some major American cities that amount of money won't buy anything at all. Recently, the average price of an apartment in New York City topped $850,000, and a house in San Francisco can be more than $650,000. That some of us end up in housing we're not crazy about is hardly surprising, given such costs. We try to beat the system, in ways large and small: We rehab old, uninspired houses, trying to put a personal stamp on them, trying to drag them into a new century. We look into modular houses, kit houses, A-frames, even mobile homes. Not a few of us are getting desperate enough to move from large cities back into the small towns and the farm country our grandparents abandoned decades ago. Some of us do find what we're looking for by these means, but many more of us do not: We settle for what some builder or other is offering and try to convince ourselves it suits us. Whether the house fits the life of its inhabitants—or the inhabitants fit their lives to the house—is often anyone's guess.

Many homebuyers want no part of these second-best strategies and accept the most onerous path to obtaining a dream house: They combine incomes, pool every conceivable resource, qualify for as much house as humanly possible, and work horrific hours to meet their mortgages. Two-story foyers, marble-countered kitchens, chandeliers and Berber carpeting are realities in these houses, not dreams. There is a price, of course, and much of that price can't be measured in dollars and cents. Mom and Dad can end up working sixty or more hours apiece, leaving no time for child rearing. To take up the slack, children are often scheduled for every after-school activity their community offers. As an unfortunate result, what should be a family can become merely a collection of people housed under one roof who meet only when their schedules permit; the effort of paying for the house controls every family dynamic found in it, and not for the better.

For those of us who want more than we have but who cannot accept any of these models into our own lives, there is another approach, not as well known as the other strategies with which we've become so wearily familiar. It's a new twist on an old theme—prefabrication—and prefabrication is not what it used to be. Whereas the goal of prefabrication was once to package an entire, hopefully ideal house, the focus has shifted. No house that can be truly mass-produced can really suit the needs of very many people: Mobile-home dwellers, for instance, often begin remodeling their houses the instant the warranty, and its sanctions against modifications, expire. Today's prefabrication is more often about prefabricating the *parts* of a house—its elements—and combining them in whatever way suits the individual needs of an owner or family.

Prefabrication might be said to be a giant game of building blocks: It is now possible to choose a foundation from one company's catalogue, walls from another, and a roof from yet another. Windows, doors, interior finishes, and amenities can be selected in the same way, and such is the array of choices that the result is not likely to be duplicated on this planet, except by intent. Everyone who can afford a house can have exactly the house that fits their needs, not someone else's idea of what a standard house might be or should be.

Today's prefab elements are available in a wide variety of price ranges as well: If the cost of one roof is more than the budget can bear, another company may make one that will be easier on the budget and look much the same. Choices of this kind do not necessarily mean that functionality or quality is sacrificed, since the technologies behind two different products can vary greatly in cost, and yet do a given job equally well. For instance, Corian costs more than Formica, yet both products yield a sanitary, water-resistant kitchen counter.

Prefab Elements is about the ways that prefabrication can give homeowners better houses, for less money. It's about companies and products. It's about architects and builders who understand that prefab elements make more house possible. It's about where prefab elements have been and where they're going.

But most of all, it's about you, and how the needs, desires, and dreams you have for your next house can be made real, one building block at a time. ▪

CHAPTER 1

history and promise

prefab **then and now**

If asked, quite a few of today's homebuyers would say they don't want a prefab house. They think of prefabrication as otherness, something alien to everyday experience. People who don't understand the principles and promise of prefabricated elements often conceptualize the end result of prefabricated approaches as a standardized, bland, sterile box that would have to have considerable customization before it would be a warm, livable home. What most people fail to realize is that prefabrication is everywhere today, and that prefabrication, not custom handwork, is what usually gives their own houses the individualized appearance and makes them prized by today's homeowners.

Today's amenities and comforts would hardly be possible for the average consumer without prefabrication. Think of present-day luxury bathrooms with their multilevel showers, capacious storage, and oversized whirlpool tubs. The tubs and showers are factory molded of sheet plastics or polyester resins; the vanities and storage cabinets are mass-produced in an infinite variety of styles and finishes. If such products were not available, there would be no choice but to do it the old way. Cabinetmakers would do the cabinetry; tile setters and masons would have to be employed for the shower and the tub. Plumbers and electricians would have to design and fabricate the whirlpool system and devise a way to conceal its machinery. Carpenters would have to make sure the floors could take a great deal of weight, and since the final weight of the installation could not be accurately predicted, some overbuilding would be necessary.

It sounds expensive, and it would be, because skilled crafts workers are always more costly than factory workers. There would also be hidden costs; the best workers make mistakes, which have to be corrected, nearly always at the expense of the client. The end result would be a bit unpredictable; it would probably look very like the plans and sketches used in its design, but adjustments and modifications would almost certainly be necessary, to compensate for problems found on the real job site.

OPPOSITE: Today's highly decorative, luxurious bathing arrangements can be composed entirely of prefab elements; a polyester resin tub surmounts steps and decking that are off-the-shelf components. Prefab window elements and moldings combine to individualize the look; the result is neither stock nor standardized.

Prefabrication takes care of every one of these problems, and more. Costs can be controlled in the factory, and the demands of the marketplace serve to cap the retail price at an affordable level. Every conceivable question can be answered before a prefab element is installed or even ordered: What *does* a whirlpool tub weigh when full of water and with an average bather? Dimensions can be controlled to tolerances seldom found in site-built work, so the promise of proper fit can be made and kept, every time. Safety is greater; a manufacturer must obtain a UL certification for an electric whirlpool unit, and provide detailed instructions for its safe installation and use. A site-built installation offers much less assurance; components individually rated for safety can be combined and used in unsafe ways. Lightweight prefab materials mean that special support construction is minimized or made unnecessary, in contrast to the heavy metal lath and concrete needed for a watertight installation using old methods. It's still possible to build the old way, and a few wealthy buyers still prefer it. They can afford to; the rest of us cannot.

OPPOSITE: Eichler houses predicted prefabrication with their modular post-and-beam construction and materials that required a minimum of on-site cutting. Many walls were sheets of quarter-inch lauan plywood fastened directly to the studs, for speed of construction and cost-effectiveness.

How did prefab elements sneak up on us and become so ubiquitous that we hardly see them for what they are? What has proved to be good—and bad—about them in the past? And if they are good, how can we extend their use, to get more for our housing dollar?

HISTORY

As recently as the 1960s, relatively few items found in the average house were prefabricated. Even the cheapest, most unassuming tract house contained plumbing screwed together and soldered by plumbers, tile set by hand, and floors nailed down one board at a time, then sanded and finished on-site. Even materials widely touted as the wave of the future were used in ways straight out of the nineteenth century. Formica was commonly cut and glued to plywood countertops by hand, in the very room where the countertop was being installed exactly as if it were wood veneer by a laborer who might or might not be making a good job of it.

Of all the major systems in older houses, only a few were customarily prefabricated: Windows led the way, alleviating a major headache for builders, and making larger, better-ventilated windows affordable for the average consumer. Oddly, in spite of the uncontested benefits of prefabricated window units, the concept took decades to spread to other systems used in housing. Doors, which come prehung in their frames today, were factorymade, but hanging them was done on-site, calling for a skilled laborer. Local subcontractors

sometimes made cabinetry for kitchens, but even as late as the 1930s, prefabricated, built-in cabinets were nearly unheard of. Most people made do with free-standing "Hoosier" units that had small cabinets below and a pull-out porcelain worktop above, more furniture than fixture. Hand-built cabinetry took care of the needs of wealthier homeowners.

Prefabricated elements entered the housing mainstream at the point where innovations usually do—the luxury end of the market. One house stands out above all others for its adventurous and pioneering use of prefabrication: Frank Lloyd Wright's magnum opus, Fallingwater, built in 1936–1937. Although Fallingwater was and is a highly individual statement, Wright achieved some of that individuality with both off-the-shelf and custom prefabrication, which he had begun to explore as early as 1902, when he spoke of the potential of prefabricated elements to improve housing. The sleekly minimalist look of Fallingwater's fenestration would not have been possible without prefabricated steel window units from Hope's, which Wright had in 1929 in his Jones House in Tulsa, Oklahoma. The windows at Fallingwater were not stock Hope's units, but they were fabricated to order from standardized parts, most of which were more commonly used in commercial construction of the time. In the house's kitchen, Wright specified a relatively new product—prefabricated, enameled-steel cabinets from St. Charles Kitchens. The company's cabinets were produced in various stock configura-tions that could be combined to produce nearly any desired result. Installation consisted mainly of bolting them into place and adding countertops to base cabinets, the way it's still done today. The yellow St. Charles Kitchens cabinets at Fallingwater look unpretentious, even ordinary now, but they were one step removed from science fiction at the time they were installed. The durability of the company's approach can be seen not only in its appropriation by many manufacturers up to the present, but in the longevity of the St. Charles Kitchens line; metal cabinetry like that at Fallingwater was produced with only minor detail changes through the 1990s.

Wright also engaged in what might be termed "custom prefabrication" at Fallingwater; he designed various cabinets and linen storage units, which were produced by the Gillen Manufacturing Company, a high-end cabinetmaking firm. Precursors of prefabricated storage components that can be bought cheaply today, Wright's units were designed to answer needs not commonly anticipated by most builders of conventional cabinetry at that time; they were of

OPPOSITE: Frank Lloyd Wright's Fallingwater made extraordinary use of prefab elements for its windows, made of stock sections normally used to create glazing for commercial structures. The vertical bank of windows at far left admits light and air to rooms on three floors.

LEFT: Inside Fallingwater, a sliding hatch made of prefab window elements provides weatherproof access to stairs that descend to the stream over which the house is built.

ABOVE: Wright used stock, prefabricated St. Charles Kitchens metal cabinets at Fallingwater; metal kitchen cabinets were a relatively new idea at the time.

nine-ply marine-grade plywood faced with walnut veneer. Linen units had shelving made of openwork, hand-woven cane. The extreme humidity occasioned by the waterfall over which the house was built made resistance to moisture a necessity. The high dimensional stability of the materials used made it possible to fit the units precisely into the stone walls of the house. Wright had foreseen today's storage and vanity units, with their waterproof surfacing over dimensionally stable substrates.

From this beginning, Wright went on to make more use of prefabrication as his career progressed; the metal window sections reappear in his Walker House of 1948 (located in Carmel, California), and many other projects. Kitchens in his houses varied tremendously, with many having custom cabinetry. But by the 1950s, his remarkable output of Usonian houses often contained prefabricated kitchen cabinets, making a pleasing contrast to his trademark rock walls and the wood details in his ceilings. As much as Wright's oeuvre benefited by prefabrication, it suffered in some places where Wright's vision surpassed

OPPOSITE: Frank Lloyd Wright's later houses, known as Usonians, featured kitchens with sleek, minimalist cabinetry intended to contrast with walls of natural wood, brick, or stone. New laminates such as Formica made sanitary countertops more affordable than older versions in hand-laid tile.

that of manufacturers. His trademark expanses of wood-framed window sometimes caused problems, as in his Archie Teater Studio in Bliss, Idaho. Wright had wanted twin-paned glass for the windows of the house, but prefabrication techniques of the era could not readily produce the parallelogram-shaped windows needed at an affordable price. The client, acting as general contractor, changed the specification to ordinary plate glass, with the result that for several decades, the house had to be closed during rigorous Idaho winters. In recent years, the house has undergone a comprehensive restoration; the owner was able to take full advantage of today's prefabrication processes, bringing the windows up to Wright's original specifications, with twin-paned glass set inside Wright's original wood framing. Thanks to improved prefabricated elements, the Teater Studio now can—and does—serve as a year-round residence. For other residential projects, where window shapes were more regular, Wright often specified prefabricated twin-pane units from companies such as Pella and Pittsburgh Plate Glass.

Other architects made use of prefabrication, of course, but usually not so well as did Wright. Indeed, some architects whose work appears to use prefabricated elements disdained the approach. Ludwig Mies van der Rohe's Farnsworth House of 1950 appears to have been built from prefabricated parts, but it is actually made largely of elements that were custom-made by hand, to an extraordinarily high standard. Mies's

ABOVE and RIGHT: Mies van der Rohe's Farnsworth House of 1950 appears to be prefabricated, but is not; its elements are handmade to extraordinary tolerances, to give a machine-made appearance. The handwork was ruinously expensive; the client sued her architect over the costs.

other buildings followed the same pattern; what appeared to be machine-made was really architectural couture, with exposed steel beams specially designed and custom fabricated to cast exactly the shadow line the architect wanted. Other International Style architects who copied Mies's work for commercial buildings often did use prefabricated elements, but not as sensitively as they might have. What was exquisitely detailed in Mies's own structures became sterile and bland when imitated by others. A more talented architect, the Californian Pierre Koenig, engaged in a form of custom prefabrication for his Case Study Houses, using stock steel framing and steel panels that were fabricated into custom sizes off-site, then assembled into a beautifully designed final structure. Charles and Ray Eames also participated in the Case Study project with a house designed for their own use; it utilized prefabricated elements in its framing and windows, resulting in an extraordinarily low cost.

The use of prefabricated elements increased somewhat in the later 1930s and the 1940s, interrupted by World War II. Many builders copied Wright's

OPPOSITE: Visionary builder Joseph Eichler wanted to offer modernist architecture to California subdivision buyers. Since some high-style features he wanted to include were not yet commercially available, Eichler prefabricated them through a subcontractor, like these kitchen cabinets with a textured finish called Zolatone.

contrast between prefabricated elements and natural materials in modified form during the postwar years. Metal kitchen cabinets began to be widely produced at many different quality levels and price points; even a modest subdivision house might get a full complement of them installed against knotty-pine-paneled walls. Wright's metal windows were also appropriated, first as steel casements, and later as aluminum-framed units that became nearly standard for 1960s housing. But 1950 was very like 1900 had been; most of the house was still built one board at a time. Change came with the housing boom of the early 1950s, for a very simple reason: There was no way to keep up with demand using old techniques. At first, builders used prefabrication very quietly, on a small scale, themselves. William J. Levitt's Levittowns were the largest-scale such effort, but Levitt actually used assembly-line techniques on his building sites more than actual off-site prefabrication. The builder-draftsman William Kesling went a bit further with his Kesling Modern Homes in California; details such as unusual kitchen cabinets were built by employees to standard plans in a small shop, then installed in the house at the proper time.

The builder Joseph Eichler did some of the most ambitious in-house prefabrication. In his mass-produced California Modern houses, specially designed, sliding-door bath and kitchen cabinets were built specifically for his houses by a subcontractor, giving an architect-designed appearance that

could not be obtained from any commercially available cabinetry of the time. By the later 1950s, mass builders had enough marketplace clout to persuade manufacturers to introduce new prefabricated products for their use; Levittowners choosing Levitt's "Country Clubber" model got a nine-and-a-half-foot-long, prefabricated GE kitchen unit in turquoise. Incorporating a combination washer-dryer, a sink with a disposal unit, a dishwasher, and a range with ventilator fan, it had a one-piece stainless steel countertop and lacked only a refrigerator, which was placed in another part of the kitchen.

But this sort of thing was still rare; the smaller local builders who constructed so much of America's mid-century housing stock were still pounding one nail at a time, fabricating most everything in their offerings on-site. Breakthroughs came slowly, but they came. One of the biggest was prefabricated kitchen cabinetry in materials other than steel; consumers who had formerly been satisfied with the utility and easy maintenance of metal units were demanding something with a warmer appearance. Once good-looking, well-made wooden cabinets in a variety of styles and finishes were readily available, they became a mainstream demand; builders couldn't very well offer a house without them. Counters followed the same path, with today's ubiquitous "postformed" design taking the place of laminate hand glued to plywood. Not only were the new counters cheaper, their molded-in backsplashes and rolled front edges

eliminated nearly all on-site fabrication. Carpenters and cabinetmakers became installers.

Much of the lure of prefabricated elements offered in the late 1950s and early 1960s was their essential modernity. Cabinets were as sleek and well finished as any major manufacturer's Danish Modern furniture, replacing the knotty pine, brushed-on varnish, and jigsawed scrolls so dear to the hearts of local cabinetmakers. Prefabricated sliding doors and bifold doors were forms not seen in older houses, which may have been more important to consumers than their supposed space-saving benefits. Fireplaces were conical metal units straight out of a *Jetsons* episode, in every glamorous color imaginable. Aluminum-framed windows became acceptable; sashes that once went only up and down suddenly could slide side to side or crank outward and upward, forming awnings that protected against rain even if nobody remembered to close them. It cannot be said that the average builder's house of this era was completely expressive of the technology of its time; distressed brick and shutters both had enormous vogues, for instance. But

OPPOSITE: By the latter half of the 1950s, prefab steel cabinets had attained a space-age sleekness; almost no warmth or home-like qualities remained. The minimalism was fashionable for a time, but a backlash would soon begin, resulting in demand for prefab period styles in wood.

for a while, the use of prefab elements ensured that a new house was patently a *new* house, This Year's Model, not to be confused with anything left over from another generation, no matter what period it aspired to. Prefabrication also made certain luxuries affordable, or at least kept their costs in line; the site-installed pine paneling so often found in earlier 1950s houses gave way to prefabricated 4-by-8-foot sheets of grooved plywood paneling by the latter part of the decade. The prized warmth of wood was no longer confined to one or two rooms; the new paneling could be used much more lavishly. The promise of "window walls," which had been so difficult to keep in earlier decades, became a reality with the introduction of stock sliding glass doors, so instantly popular as to become almost a standard amenity by 1970.

One house in Houston stands as a tribute to the achievements of prefabrication in the 1960s; it is a townhouse built as part of a three-unit cluster designed by Talbott Wilson and Hal Weatherford of Wilson Morris Crain and Anderson Architects for the 1969 National Home Builders Show. Intended to showcase

OPPOSITE: In 1969, General Electric and a Houston electric utility collaborated on the "Style in Steel Townhouses," a "dream house" showcase for total electric living. Recently restored by new owners, the units featured prefabricated, sliding window wall units set in steel framing.

products manufactured by General Electric, the steel-framed townhouses incorporated many prefab elements. Twelve-foot sliding glass walls gave each unit views of a system of courtyards; prefabricated closet units looked forward to today's flexible storage. Prefab cabinets graced the kitchens, and prefab panels were used on bathroom walls, eliminating much of the tile setting still common at the time. Called the "Style in Steel Townhouses," the units were the hit of the builders' show and have been recently restored by owners who appreciate their International Style heritage. Intriguingly, the prefab elements in the houses have survived as well as, if not better than, elements that were site built. Clearly, prefabrication caused no loss of quality in these upscale units.

By the latter part of the 1960s, though, a certain amount of backlash against modernism was beginning to manifest itself in consumer choices. Flush doors, unadorned surfaces, and the frank use of synthetics were suddenly much less popular than before, victims of a mass market that wanted to be somehow up-to-date and down-home at the same time. Manufacturers responded by adding panels to doors, faking mullions in their aluminum windows, and lavishing "wood-grain" vinyl on everything in sight, including paneling. Very few of these new prefabricated elements were entirely successful at evoking past eras; they were very little more than ersatz substitutes for skilled craft work that had become unaffordable. By the 1970s, a new subdivision house had

LEFT and ABOVE: The "Style in Steel Townhouses" made extensive use of prefabricated cabinetry in their kitchens, bathrooms, and closet areas. These units are original to the townhouses; they have served since 1969 with only minimal repair and refurbishment.

very few natural materials in evidence; paradoxically, the appearance of natural materials was highly prized. Vinyl flooring emulated Spanish tile; injection-molded plastics copied hand-hewn beams and even brick walls. None of it would have fooled any but the most self-delusional consumer, but it was snapped up anyway, largely because it was all that any but the most affluent home buyer could get.

The 1980s brought a new backlash; the artifice of the 1970s began to be seen as tacky and passé. Younger consumers who had been brought up with the Brady Bunch look began demanding a more "honest" and traditional appearance in their housing. Although a certain amount of craftsmanship was revived, mainstream consumer demand for perceived honesty was met as much by better fakery as it was with handmade products. Window manufacturers made remarkable progress; they began by painting and cladding their products in ways that made them more closely resemble traditional units. Ultimately, prefabricated windows were invented that took full advantage of technology with aluminum and vinyl, but with delicate shadow lines in their traditionally

OPPOSITE: Laminate flooring is one of the newest prefab elements; it permits busy homeowners to have the luxurious look of wood without the high maintenance requirements of the real thing. The product is designed for do-it-yourself installation.

profiled mullions and framing. Doors followed much the same pattern, this time in high-security steel stamped with panels that copied eighteenth-century models. Even that symbol of suburban wretchedness, vinyl siding, was vastly improved, with a weathered-wood texture becoming nearly standard; beading enhanced the profiles of better lines. By the 1990s, it was possible for a sensitive, well-informed architect to reproduce, with great visual fidelity, period house styles using prefab elements. A time traveler from old Williamsburg might easily pass one of today's better-cloned Colonials without noticing anything particularly odd about it, except perhaps the unusually regular appearance of its vinyl millwork.

Consumers interested in period architecture today are much more selective than formerly about what constitutes acceptable artifice in prefab elements; exterior materials are usually synthetic now, but in interiors, natural materials are demanded in most areas of all but the cheapest housing. Prefabricated cabinets are now back to real wood, with period styling and detailing that is sometimes artificially distressed to appear old. In the interiors of today's traditional-style houses, synthetics are tolerated primarily in three places—countertops, bathroom elements, and flooring. Today's prefabricated laminate flooring, such as Pergo, makes it possible for busy wage earners to have wood-look floors without the trouble of caring for real wood or the expense of hiring to have it done. Prefabricated countertops are

available in polyester-based materials such as Corian that offer advantages even stone cannot match: If you chip a Corian countertop, it can be repaired nearly invisibly. Bath and shower enclosures don't even make an effort to look like tile or marble; for some reason, their high-tech look is acceptable, even for consumers who insist on natural materials elsewhere in the same room. The old 1970s esthetic of cladding everything in vinyl printed to look like wood survives primarily in lower-end housing and in mobile homes.

Today modernism is back with a vengeance. Many baby boomers who grew up in modernist tract housing and participated in the backlash against it have revived their affection for its clean lines and easy-care detailing. A new generation with no prejudices also finds the modernist esthetic appealing. Many consumers under 35 are far more familiar with the works of Frank Lloyd Wright, Richard Neutra, Ludwig Mies van der Rohe, and Pierre Koenig than are their elders, who were around when these architects' iconic houses were new. Of all the consumers who are building houses today, this generation stands to benefit most from the promise of prefabricated elements. No fakery is needed when designing a house that hews to no past tradition; even the newest and most unusual prefab elements are perfectly suited to modernism. Today's prefabricated products make it possible for

LEFT: Today's prefabricated kitchen cabinets are available with a warm, handcrafted appearance, though they're just as efficient as mid-century metal cabinets. Even custom door panels for refrigerator doors and dishwasher fronts are stock elements.

newly built modernism to fulfill promises of the style that formerly could not be kept. For example, a truly waterproof membrane for a flat roof can be rapidly unrolled and fastened at the roof edges, completely bypassing the problems of older tar-and-gravel systems. Glass walls no longer require indentured servitude to a energy supplier; prefabricated twin-pane units keep weather in its place. The very foundation on which a house sits can be trucked to site, its sections craned into place; it can withstand moisture and cold much better than anything from the past.

Prefab elements can contribute to the most experimental and radical architecture. Bart Prince is one of the most innovative architects in America, yet he appreciates what prefab elements can do to give his residential projects unusual forms and great cost effectiveness. Prince is a leading exponent of the principles of organic architecture as formulated by Frank Lloyd Wright; Prince learned the fundamentals of applying prefabrication to his designs from his mentor, Bruce Goff, who was trained by Wright himself. Although Wright was perfectly comfortable with prefab elements up to a point, he tended to seek out elements whose purpose was already defined and to use them for that intended purpose. Goff's contribution to the use of prefab elements was to look for elements that could serve purposes that their creators

RIGHT: Organic architect Bart Prince designed the Gradow Residence using prefab window elements that follow the curving walls of the pod-like bays that step down the hillside on which the house is built. What was intended for commercial use has become art.

never envisioned; his Ford House was constructed of parts scavenged from a Quonset hut.

Bart Prince continues this tradition, looking everywhere for prefab elements that can be used in ways that enrich the design of a house, instead of "dumbing down" its concept. Two of his built projects show his approach; each uses prefab elements in very different ways to suit two very different clients. His Gradow Residence is a 40,000-square-foot house in a resort area, intended by its owners to be a highly individual expression. The request for a very large house was not easy to fulfill; such a house is often an imposition on its site, a bulk that has no relation to the land on which it sits. Such a bulk would have been the antithesis of organic architecture, which seeks to integrate buildings fully with their surroundings. Prince's solution was to build the house in several large "pod" formations that cascade gently down the site's slope. Each pod cantilevered over the one below it; the house is shaped by its site.

One of the most striking uses of prefab elements in the Gradow Residence is in its glass curtain-wall elements, more commonly found in commercial construction. Instead of being flat windows in flat walls, they repeat the curves of each "pod." The resulting huge arcs of glass do much more than permit a

LEFT: Each pod of the Gradow Residence is cantilevered over the one below it; the gentle, rhythmic cascade of forms belies the house's enormous size—40,000 square feet. Creative use of prefab elements throughout the structure made it affordable.

peek outdoors; they sweep around the house's occupants, demolishing the feeling of enclosure found in most houses. As a result, nature is not merely observed from the house; instead, it is experienced. The change of seasons and each day's weather are part of the owners' lives, not second-hand information that can be ignored in favor of other pursuits. Even the dangers of nature are experienced, from a safe remove. A magnificent storm can inspire exhilaration when seen from the shelter of the house, because the window area puts the viewer out in the storm while still offering protection from it.

Another Bart Prince project is nearly antithetical to the Gradow Residence. Called the Parsifal Townhomes, it is a low-rise condominium development in Albuquerque, New Mexico. The land on which it is built is desert, only modestly sloped, with little character. Another architect might have turned out a series of boxes similar to others nearby, but Prince has used prefab elements to turn commerce into art. His trapezoidal plan for each unit offers spaces that are reasonably familiar, yet possessing a difference that intrigues and breaks out of the sterility of the box. Sloped elements on the exteriors relate the buildings to Albuquerque's topography, making reference to the eroded sides of desert rock formations.

RIGHT: Bart Prince's Parsifal Townhomes in Albuquerque, New Mexico form a speculative housing development built with prefab elements. The stock garage doors were designed for service stations, but they become sleek contemporary architecture in this residential setting.

When Bart Prince designed the Gradow Residence, the luxurious budget for the project meant that some of its prefab elements could be customized, special-ordered variations from the factory. For Parsifal, Prince respected the budget of a speculative development by using what he refers to as "stock-out-of-the-box" cabinetry, doors, and windows. Parsifal's garages were kept from being bland and faceless by the use of glazed garage doors more commonly associated with service stations. Not only do they lend great visual interest to the exteriors of the townhomes, their commercial associations are entirely eliminated by the skill with which they are used. A condominium at Parsifal Townhomes can be bought for less than $200,000, but the principles guiding its design are the same as in Prince's custom houses.

OLD AND NEW

Even those who are not looking for, or building, a new house can benefit from prefabricated elements. An older house's roof can receive a traditional tiled appearance. The new roof can be installed quickly, in lightweight panels that don't require beefed-up roof trusses. The same prefabricated foundation that supports new houses can replace a faulty old foundation. Everyone is familiar with prefabricated replacement windows and doors; old, leaking windows can be banished in favor of units that keep weather outdoors, and utility bills low. Today's doors are much more secure and energy efficient than anything from the past.

But it is in new houses that prefab elements offer the greatest promise: You can prefab a house from the ground up, picking and choosing what suits your needs, taste, and circumstances. Your house can be built more quickly, last longer, cost less. All you have to do is to ask yourself the question, who makes this element in prefab form? ■

OPPOSITE and **ABOVE**: Builder-designer Patrick Seabol has begun to build new steel-and-glass houses in Palm Springs, where such architecture has been popular for decades. The prefab window walls seen here look like mid-century units, but do much more to keep sun and heat out of the house.

ABOVE: Seabol's Palm Springs houses are designed to give younger buyers the prized look of mid-century architecture at an affordable price. OPPOSITE, ABOVE and BELOW: The builder uses stock prefab window, door, fireplace, and cabinet elements for cost-effectiveness; finishes are minimal, so buyers can choose their own.

prefab elements

putting it together

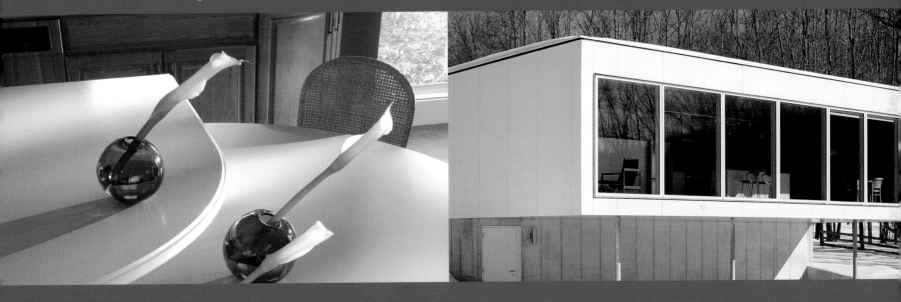

a selection of prefab elements

A house is the largest and most complex object most of us will ever own. So mystifying are the workings of houses to most owners that they tend to look only at the surface of the structure, content to rely on warranties, luck, and assumptions that everything under the skin is of good quality and will continue to work properly. Such complacency is often workable for those in existing houses—after all, the house stands and its systems are usually in working order. Those who are building must face a series of decisions, large and small, all of which will affect the outcome of the building process. One poorly selected component can not only become unsatisfactory in its own right, it can also affect the performance of other elements that must work in conjunction with it.

With so many decisions to be made, it's easy for someone building a house to become overwhelmed. Without research and preparation, the process becomes frenzied; no sooner does the owner decide one issue than another presents itself. The time to decide what elements you want for your house is before a line is drawn by the architect. If the owner decides that certain products are desirable, then everyone concerned can design and work with those requirements in mind.

When planning to use prefab elements, it's helpful to think in terms of the major systems of a house, to determine what will be used in each, and then to resolve any potential conflicts between elements in different systems. An example would be choosing prefab glazing elements to be inserted into a prefab wall system: Can the glazing be installed in a panel of the particular material used? Is the panel thick enough to accept the framing of the glazing element? Careful research is needed. It may take months of poring over manufacturer Web sites, brochures, and product drawings, but eliminating incompatibilities at this stage pays large dividends, since doing so now is cost free. Later will be too late. A truckload of wall panels that will not work with the chosen foundation or roof systems will cost a fortune to return, if they're returnable at all.

Here is a selection of prefab elements for each of the major systems in a house, as well as a shortcut prefab means of adding onto an existing dwelling. ■

OPPOSITE: Prefab window, door, and glass block elements are visible here, but the foundation on which the house sits, as well as its floor system, walls, and roof, can be prefabricated as well.

foundations & floor structures

A foundation seems to be simple enough: A house must rest on something, and that something should be very sturdy, in addition to being resistant to movement. Those are important considerations, but there is much more to a foundation than simple weight-bearing requirements. Today's foundations are at the core of a house's longevity and its energy usage. Older, site-built systems—such as concrete-block foundation walls built in a trench extending below a site's frostline—are still very much in use. They are easy to build, and most builders are very comfortable with this technology. Few owners worry about anything more than having a dry basement, free of cracks in its walls. It's too bad that more owners don't investigate prefab foundation systems, because such elements can deliver all the traditional virtues of expensive site-built foundations, and more. It is even possible to have a foundation that has minimal impact on the land, or for temporary structures, or to protect a sensitive site.

Prefab foundation walls can be better protected against leakage, since water-resistant materials can be incorporated into them at the time of manufacture, under controlled conditions. A site-built foundation usually relies on the experience and judgment of the builder, who must decide on a combination of waterproofing materials and drainage, and entrust the execution of his ideas to workers who may or may not do their jobs in the manner intended. With prefab foundation elements, the panel structure can include insulation. This idea has many benefits. If the basement is to be finished, it will be easier to keep heated. If unfinished, it will still be warmer than an uninsulated basement, protecting plumbing and other systems and adding to the overall energy efficiency of the completed house. It can easily be seen that living spaces located over an insulated basement capable of holding a temperature of 55 degrees will be cheaper to heat than ones over an uninsulated basement in the same climate, with a temperature of 40 degrees.

One company that combines traditional basement materials with prefab technology is Kistner Concrete Products. The firm's Thermal-Krete system of precast concrete panels is intended to perform all the preceding tasks. Thermal-Krete also has advantages. Thermal-Krete panels are self-contained; their high strength means that they can be installed in a foundation trench on a bed of compacted gravel, instead of the poured-concrete footer required for concrete block foundations. Concrete-block construction includes 5,000 psi (pounds per square inch; a measure of strength) concrete, reinforced with rebar, steel reinforcing rods that are embedded in the concrete. The Thermal-Krete panel design includes a molded-in header, a footer, and reinforcing ribs. These elements do not have to be added on site, and this monolithic structure also ensures that every element adds to panel strength. Two inches of polyurethane insulation are foamed in place during manufacture; the process also adds steel studs to which interior wall finishes can be attached.

Installation of a Thermal-Krete foundation is much faster than building a traditional concrete-block foundation, or even one built of poured concrete. Once excavation is completed, panels are craned into place, one at a time. As each is installed, a polyurethane adhesive is applied to the connecting faces of each panel, and the panels are fastened together with steel hardware. The result is a structure much stronger than either block or poured-concrete systems. Waterproofing is done after the entire foundation has set, with a polyurethane-membrane "wrap" that works together with the inherent water-resistance of such high-strength concrete. Normally 4,000 psi concrete is considered water-resistant in its own right; the combination of the 5,000 psi concrete in the Thermal-Krete system plus the "wrap" yields basement walls with a high margin of protection against water intrusion. The product comes in several stock sizes, to accommodate needs for different basement wall heights. The three-foot height serves for most houses built over a crawl space, and the eight-foot height works for most full basements. Other panel lengths are available up to 18 feet by special order.

Although most traditional-style houses have had prefab wooden floor-joist systems for many years, steel joists are gaining in popularity for residential use. Houses have become larger, with dwellings of 4,000 square feet and more gaining in popularity. Currently fashionable interior finish materials are often surprisingly heavy—marble or terracotta floors are frequent selections. Other heavy elements such as oversized whirlpool tubs and professional ranges add greatly to the weight-bearing requirements of a floor's structure. Marino\WARE's Joist-RITE steel floor joists, among many other steel products, can help create a house capable of accepting enormous floor loads. Joist-RITE joists are a pressed-steel product engineered with large, open triangular sections running

ABOVE: A pneumatic hammer is used to drive pins through a Diamond Pier pin foundation; the concrete foundation element rests on the surface, but is pinned to the ground at a point below the frost line. OPPOSITE: Diamond Piers can be used for permanent or temporary structures, like this Edgar Blazona design.

down each joist, like the triangles seen in bridge trusses. These sections both contribute to strength—a triangle is very difficult to deform—and allow easy installation of other elements such as wiring and plumbing. When a wire or pipe comes to a joist, the installer doesn't need to stop and drill through it; the pipe or wire—or even a heating duct—can simply be passed through one of the open triangles.

Joist-RITE is inherently fire resistant, able to survive a blaze without collapse, and does not support microorganisms that contribute to black mold or other allergy-provoking situations. The open triangular sections also help the product resist transmission of sound and cold temperatures; they simply have less mass to become chilled and pass the cold to the floor surface above the joists. Since houses are all different, one Joist-RITE product does not fit all; Marino\WARE produces various sizes of the joists to accommodate any weight that might be placed on a floor. Since the product requires engineering calculations for many projects, Marino\WARE offers design services, creating complete, detailed engineering drawings in AutoCAD computer-assisted design format. Technical assistance is also available by phone, fax, or e-mail. Builders who have used a steel joist system before are able to adapt to using Joist-RITE easily. The company's installation guides show how it can be combined with other common construction materials to create a complete structure. In addition to floor joists, the company makes wall- and roof-framing products using the same concept and having the same benefits.

Sometimes a foundation does not need to be a heavy, monolithic structure. A house might be located where a traditional foundation might interfere with water runoff in ways detrimental to the area. A vacation house in a remote location might need a foundation that does not require heavy materials trucked in over long distances. And a building might be temporary: Why not build a simple house today and remove it tomorrow to build a more ambitious one when circumstances permit? One solution that meets these needs is Pin Foundations's Diamond Pier, a patented system that permits a foundation to be installed almost anywhere, inexpensively, easily, with minimal impact to the site. Diamond Piers, named for the diamond shape of their concrete elements, are installed by placing the pier in a shallow hole dug in the ground, and driving steel pins through the pier to extend deep into the earth. The concrete is thereby "pinned" to the site by the steel, which extends below the frost line, the depth to which the ground freezes in winter. (The frost line varies by geographic location; anyone needing to know the frost-line depth in their area should check with their county's extension service.) A metal bracket on top of the concrete element permits the framing of the house to be bolted to it.

Diamond Piers can be installed by driving the pins manually with sledgehammers with pneumatic

automatic driving hammer. The number and length of pins can be varied accordingly to deal with site conditions; piers are available in two sizes for different weight-bearing requirements. Once all the Diamond Piers needed for a building are set, the exposed heads of their pins are protected against corrosion with caps, which are covered with a silicone sealant. Although most pier systems rely on a base of concrete poured into a hole excavated to a level below the frost line, Diamond Piers do not. The system rides the surface, pinned to solid ground below the frost line by the steel pins. If the surface of the ground is heaved by frost, the ground is cleft aside by the diamond shape of the concrete pier as it pushes upward, leaving the pier itself undisturbed. Pin Foundations also makes a wall system using some of the same principles as Diamond Piers. This system creates concrete walls that are pinned to the ground, so that the high-load-bearing properties of such a wall can be obtained without excavation. Diamond Pier's low site impact and ease of installation have made it a choice of the designer Edgar Blazona,

OPPOSITE: This hilly lot would have required massively obtrusive, expensive foundation walls if conventional techniques had been used. Topsider Homes's pedestal foundation system supports a house without encumbering the land upon which it sits, visually or physically.

whose Modular Dwellings prefabricated rooms and houses are often installed using the system.

In many areas of the United States, building lots are at a premium; most major cities are so heavily built up that the few remaining lots tend to be the least desirable, sloping and hilly. Topsider Homes has a solution for this problem—the pedestal foundation. A pedestal foundation is easy to understand; it's something like the stem of a mushroom, with the house sitting on top of it and extending outward from it, like the mushroom's cap. Since the foundation is much smaller than the house, it is usually much easier to find sufficient area on a difficult lot for a pedestal foundation than for a traditional one. Formerly a concept found mainly in expensive, architect-designed houses (the architect Bart Prince's Gradow Residence uses the idea), pedestal foundations are now a design within the reach of many homeowners. The Topsider system is not available separately from the company's houses, which are prefabricated using post-and-beam construction, but Topsider will design a completely custom house; homeowners are not limited to stock designs.

Topsider handles its custom design projects from beginning to end; the client is interviewed and a house designed around the needs and desires expressed at that time. Plans and architectural drawings are done, and Topsider assists in letting out bids with builders it has recruited in the client's area. Assistance is also given with building permits,

and financing can be found for qualified buyers who do not have a lender in mind. Through use of its prefabrication technologies, Topsider is able to take a custom house project from dream to reality in as little as four and a half months, including all design, prefabrication, delivery, and building time. For homeowners who don't need a custom design, standard design packages are available, shortening the time needed to produce a house. Not every Topsider design uses a pedestal foundation—many of company's designs are very traditional in appearance—but the pedestal design produces a house that floats over its lot, giving a sense of space and freedom few conventional house designs can match.

Anyone building a foundation must provide drainage for it; basements and crawl spaces collect water with appalling efficiency if their drainage systems are not properly designed, installed, and maintained. Tremco Barrier Solutions's DrainStar Stripdrain system replaces traditional tile-and-gravel drains around foundation walls; the company claims a lower total cost and easier installation for the system, as compared with gravel. Much of the cost savings comes in the form of savings on shipping; the components for a typical DrainStar installation are much lighter than the gravel that would be needed for the same job. DrainStar consists of rectangular polymer panels that frame a series of conical polymer elements; these do the same job as gravel, collecting water and moving it toward the exit point defined during the installation.

DrainStar overcomes one of gravel's most severe drawbacks—soil compaction. Gravel is supposed to create an area in the soil around a house where water can flow freely through the spaces between each stone, to be draining away from the foundation. However, when soil excavated from the site of a foundation is replaced around its completed walls, the soil begins working its way into the spaces needed for water flow. The problem increases with each passing rain, since water carries more soil into the spaces, becoming more firmly compacted with time. DrainStar ameliorates this problem with a filter of non-woven fabric that keeps fine soil out of the spaces between its polymer cones. DrainStar is intended for use with two other Tremco products. WATCHDOG WATERPROOFING is a seamless membrane that is sprayed onto the outer walls of the foundation to create resistance to hydrostatic pressure, caused by groundwater pressing on the walls of a foundation from outside. TUFF-N-DRI, a water-resistant foundation board combined with a spray-on seamless membrane, is designed for applications where moisture and condensation, rather than hydrostatic pressure, are a problem. Matched to one of the other products, the DrainStar system can keep a basement genuinely dry, with greater reliability over its service life. Tremco's products can be retrofitted to existing houses, providing the foundation can be sufficiently exposed by excavation. ■

OPPOSITE: Pedestal foundation systems can put a house out of reach of potential flooding. ABOVE: Pedestal foundations also permit the land underneath a house to be used as outdoor space. Such prefab elements can give homeowners much more safety, savings, and pleasure for their money than older technologies did.

walls

Walls—outer walls, that is—are one of the most labor-intensive and failure-prone systems in a house. In traditional construction, they are framed with wood, with each piece cut to length on the job site, then nailed together. When framing is completed, the walls must be equipped with a vapor barrier to stop penetration of moisture into the house, with insulation to keep cold and heat out of it, and must be clad inside and out with finish materials. The outside can be anything from wood or vinyl siding to brick or stucco; the inside is usually finished with Sheetrock. The multiplicity of processes means that the cost of such construction has always been very high; one team of workers after another must go over a wall several times to complete it.

The performance of the completed wall has always depended on several factors hard for a home-owner to judge: the quality of the materials used, the

appropriateness of the materials selected, and the quality of the workmanship needed for each step. Very simple mistakes, such as installing a vapor barrier on the wrong side of sheathing materials, can contribute to poor energy efficiency, black mold infestations, and even rotting of the wall. Companies that prefabricate walls generally use the same basic concept, called a structural insulated panel, or SIP. However, not all SIPs are created equal, and that's not mere ad-speak. Different brands of SIPs are made of various materials using several basic technologies, allowing a choice of the best material for a given structure. In the Northeast, a SIP clad with a wood product will generally perform very satisfactorily. But in the drier parts of Southern California, where brush fires are increasingly common, a SIP that can be faced in fireproof materials may be the only feasible choice in an especially risky area. SIPs are not just for walls; they make excellent roof panels when fastened to roof trusses, yielding an insulated roof deck in one installation step, ready for finish roofing.

Better Building Systems produces a classic SIP that is faced inside and out with a wood product called oriented strand board (OSB) and has a wood header and footer. The inner core of the panel is expanded

polystyrene foam with a high insulating value; panels are treated with a nontoxic borax compound for termite resistance. The edge of the panel has OSB flanges that align each panel with its neighbor. Constructing a wall is a simple matter of lifting a panel into place, aligning it so that the flange fits the mating edge of the next panel, and fastening the panel to the floor and adjoining panels. Since each panel is self-supporting, framing requirements are greatly reduced; only such areas as roofs, doors, and windows must be framed or given trusses. Exterior and interior finishes can be applied over the panels quickly and easily, since their entire inner and outer faces are suitable for nailing.

Although OSB itself has many advantages, Better Building Systems's panel construction is not the whole story. The company produces panel packages for complete houses, including every panel shape required for even the most complex design. Panels are coded so that the assembly process follows a sequence familiar to anyone who has ever assembled gingerbread cutouts into a miniature house. The company offers a series of standard houses, called Nature House designs complete with everything needed to construct a finished exterior shell. After erection of the shell, the interiors of a Nature House can be finished to the owner's specifications, using standard

ABOVE, LEFT and RIGHT: SIPs are fitted together to form the walls of a house, then prefabricated roof trusses are added to support the roof decking and roofing. OPPOSITE: The result is a house that looks completely conventional, yet costs less to build and yields energy savings.

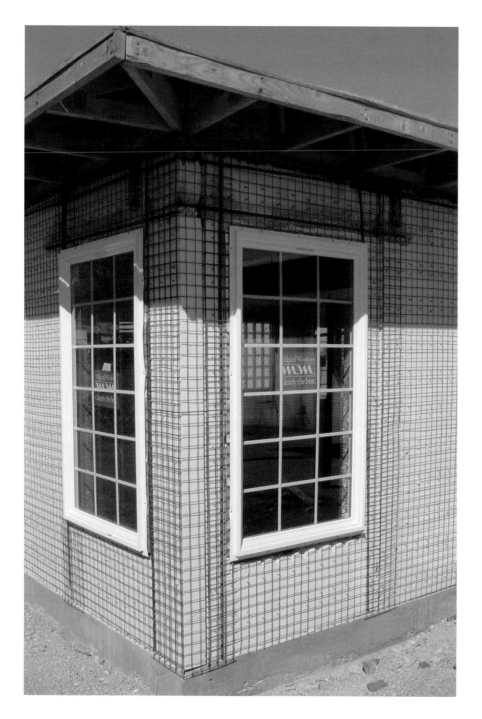

drywalling techniques and traditional finish materials. BBS can also produce panels for houses designed by a homeowner's chosen architect, or the two architects on its staff can custom-design a house, which is then panelized and delivered to the job site for assembly. The design process includes locating all chases (recesses) intended to contain wiring and plumbing in each panel; finished panels are ready to begin accepting utility runs as soon as they are erected.

A very different approach is taken by Hadrian Tridi-Systems, with its Tridipanel SIP. Tridipanel uses no wood in its construction. The system consists of a steel "space frame" made of inner and outer wire-mesh panels that hold the panels together and provide strength. In addition, diagonal truss wires keep the inner and outer panels at a distance from each other, and give added strength. Polystyrene insulation is foamed in place between the inner and outer mesh panels; the diagonal truss wires run through the insulation, so that the entire panel becomes a structural unit. A very small amount of space is left between the polystyrene core and the mesh faces to facilitate installation of surface finishes. Ron Hadrian, the owner of Hadrian Tridi-Systems, says that the usual finish for a Tridipanel house is shotcrete, concrete sprayed onto the surface of the panels. Properly applied shotcrete flows into the space between the polystyrene core and the wire mesh and also surrounds the mesh, burying it under a monolithic surface of concrete. This makes for an exceptionally strong construction. Tridipanels are perhaps the most fire-resistant SIP available, often being specified for commercial construction, where fire codes are much more stringent than for residential construction.

Although shotcrete produces a very attractive, stucco-like finish, that look is not for everyone, so Hadrian has devised methods by which Tridipanels can accept almost any interior or exterior finish. Wood studs can be fastened to the wire mesh with wire ties; shotcrete can then be applied to the wall and troweled flush with the studs, leaving their faces exposed. Traditional finish materials such as wood or vinyl siding can then be nailed to the studs. Chases for utilities are easy to form; Hadrian recommends using a torch to "cut" chases into the polystyrene core. The flame is passed along the surface of the panel before a wall finish is applied, and the polystyrene melts in its wake, leaving a recess into which wiring and pipes can be inserted. After the installation of utilities, the interior wall surface is finished, concealing the chases. Tridipanel can be cut into complex shapes such as archways and corbels with a reciprocating saw and bolt cutter; window and door openings also are cut by this means.

A SIP with a very high insulating value is needed in the Northeast, and Ray-Core makes one that is ideally suited to that climate. Ray-Core's SIPs are made of expanded polystyrene and include wood studs spaced 16 inches on center; the panel is almost *all* insulation. Wall panels are three-and-a-half inches thick and four feet wide. They come in several lengths,

OPPOSITE: Hadrian Tridipanels are SIPs with a steel support structure and foam insulation. ABOVE: When finished with a sprayed-on concrete called shotcrete, they form a highly fire-resistant structure. Other, more traditional finishes can easily be applied to Tridipanels as well.

with the longest being nine feet. The wood studs permit fast and easy finishing inside and out. Each edge of a Ray-Core panel is formed to create a shiplap joint; the joints interlock to minimize air infiltration between panels. During installation, a bead of construction adhesive is applied to the edges, securing the panels and completing the seal between them. Great cost savings are possible at every stage of construction with Ray-Core panels. The panels are easy to cut with common construction tools and easy to install, making fast construction possible. An eight-foot panel weighs only 43 pounds, creating lower shipping costs than would be possible for the materials needed for traditional construction. One worker can handle one panel quite easily, cutting labor costs.

Ray-Core also offers roof panels whose construction differs somewhat from the Ray-Core wall panel. Measuring five-and-a-half inches thick to prevent heat loss, roof panels have a fiberglass-reinforced foil applied to both sides, creating a radiant vapor barrier. The barrier does not allow moisture to pass through the panel, and the foil finish reflects heat. On the upper side of the panel, the foil barrier reflects the sun's rays, so that heat loads are reduced in the summer. On its lower side, the panel's foil reflects the house's heat back into the house, reducing heating costs in winter. Panels are available in eight- or ten-foot lengths and weigh no more than 60 pounds, making for greater handling safety, essential when working at roof level. Once Ray-Core roof panels are in place, any roofing system that can be applied over wood studs can be used.

One wall requirement that does not usually use a SIP is one with which today's new homeowners are becoming all too familiar: the retaining wall. As was mentioned earlier, in many major cities, every level building lot was snapped up long ago. Most available lots require some ingenuity when building on them. Many hilly or sloping lots require stabilization with retaining walls. Although Hadrian's Tridipanel system can be used for some lighter retaining walls, many retaining walls are called on to hold back substantial masses of earth, requiring them to be heavy and resistant to movement. One product capable of doing the job almost anywhere is Redi-Rock International's Redi-Rock large-block retaining wall system. Made of high-strength concrete, installed Redi-Rock walls appear to be made of quarried stone cut in pieces. Only when a block is seen out of context is the product's secret revealed: What seems to be many pieces of stone is one massive precast unit, weighing an average of 1,500 pounds. Redi-Rock comes in different sizes and configurations to create walls of different shapes.

OPPOSITE: The Redi-Rock retaining wall seen opposite appears to have been built the traditional way, of small stone blocks laid by masons. It is actually composed of large blocks whose faces appear to be many smaller blocks, saving construction time and money.

OPPOSITE: Redi-Rock comes in a wide array of stock elements that can be combined in different arrangements to create a custom-laid, traditional masonry appearance.
ABOVE, LEFT and RIGHT: Curved walls, stairs, planting spaces, and freestanding walls are easily achieved with the system.

Each Redi-Rock is designed to interlock, with Lego-like bumps and recesses that mate when the blocks are forklifted into place.

Redi-Rock is suitable for both low and tall retaining walls. Taller installations can require a mesh called geo-grid to be buried in the earth behind the wall, with some of the mesh allowed to extend from the earth; this free end of the mesh is sandwiched between the blocks as they are stacked during installation. This fastens the wall securely to the bank of soil behind it. The company offers design services; AutoCAD drawings of all its block configurations are available online to assist architects who need to incorporate it into their projects. In addition to the quarried limestone look, a cobblestone look is available; Redi-Rock can also custom-color the concrete used in its product. Since the blocks are very heavy, Redi-Rock is made to stringent company specifications by its network of dealers; the dealers are well spaced across most of the United States, so that shipping distances and costs are minimized. Redi-Rock performs frequent quality checks to be certain that the company's specifications are adhered to.

OPPOSITE: An Arctic shelter on Ellesmere Island was built by scientists who lived in it during an expedition. Experienced builders were not needed, due to the simplicity of SIP construction. The Thermapan SIPs used kept the building warm in temperatures as low as -76 degrees Fahrenheit.

Anyone wanting to build with SIPs in very cold climates needs to use SIPs designed for extreme conditions. Canadian-made, Thermapan SIPs have been used successfully in the Arctic; a scientific expedition's base on Ellesmere Island was built with the product. The SIPs made it possible for the scientists involved to erect the 1,900-square-foot structure themselves in only three weeks, without the help of experienced builders. Although Thermapan SIPs look somewhat similar to those of other brands, with their wood-product faces and polystyrene cores, the company's panels were able to keep the expedition team warm in temperatures as cold as -76 degrees Fahrenheit. Heating-fuel consumption was significantly lower than the team had anticipated; the heat could actually be left off for some hours without danger of freezing temperatures occurring inside the structure.

Thermapan is also noted for its strength, a great asset when heavy snow loads are involved. The ease of building with SIPs is of great benefit to one of the company's pet projects, Habitat for Humanity houses. SIPs are donated or supplied at cost by Thermapan to several Habitat chapters. Unskilled volunteers use them to build Habitat dwellings. The volunteers, often trained by other volunteers who have been building only a short time, are able to erect houses quickly and easily with the SIPs. The Habitat clients who eventually own the houses get more than just an affordable mortgage payment; the energy efficiency of the Thermapan system keeps their heating costs low as well. ▪

glazing

Houses need light and air, but today's glazing has advanced far beyond the traditional double-hung window set deeply into a vertical wall. New advances in materials and manufacturing techniques make it possible to pierce the outer skin of a house almost anywhere, without water leakage or massive energy costs. At one time energy efficiency meant that glazing elements looked somewhat high-tech, less than suited to traditional architecture. That era has ended: Windows and other glazing are now available in very traditional looks. The best traditionally styled products have gotten so good that they pass close inspection when correctly installed. Their frames and mullions are wood; they are properly recessed into the façade of a house; and their present-day specialty hardware (such as locks that permit tilting of a window sash into the room for cleaning) is unobtrusive. Only a look at the edges of the glass where it meets the mullions gives away the secret of the double panes found in today's windows.

On the modernist front, many exciting innovations are available. Today's urethane gaskets make glass walls practical; older modernist structures had the glass, but not the double panes and airtight seal that are standard now. Skylight technology has advanced far beyond the days of water leaks, heat buildup from excessive sun, and the notorious siphoning off of heat that used to occur in winter months.

Glazing technology has made entirely new rooms possible in mainstream housing: Conservatories and sunrooms that are usable year round are now within reach of many owners who could not have afforded them—or their heating and cooling requirements—in the past. Installation of prefab glazing elements is simpler than ever before; new framing technologies provide leak-free service without complicated flashing requirements. There used to be plenty of good reasons to have conventional windows that are limited in area to minimize heat leakage in winter. Those days are gone.

Prefab skylights were *the* wonder housing product of the 1950s; many architectural photographs of the period show modernist houses proudly sporting them in rows and clusters. They were especially

OPPOSITE: This conservatory appears to have been built by traditional methods, yet is prefabricated for ease of installation and cost savings. High-tech glazing makes it energy efficient; older conservatory designs could require a lot of supplemental heat in cold months.

pleasing when viewed at night, from outside; their bubble-of-light look punctuated and embellished slab-roofed architecture that might otherwise have appeared bland. The look came at a price; one 1960s socialite who had the idea of brightening her mammoth walk-in closets with skylights found that the shoulders of her Diors and Balenciagas faded within weeks. The performance of older skylights was limited by two major factors: Sealing gaskets depended on synthetic rubber formulas that were not as good as today's, and no one had yet thought to double the plastic dome itself, creating a thermal break between an inner and outer dome that conserved energy.

All these problems—and more—have been resolved. Companies such as Solar Innovations and Solatube have created skylights that promote today's standards of energy efficiency and comfort; new designs never envisioned in the mid-century era are available. Solatube's approach to skylights is unique and versatile: The company's products use a tube lined with reflective material between the roof dome and the diffuser mounted in the ceiling. Because of the tube, no expensive framing is needed, since the skylight shaft used by most skylights is not present. One hole in the roof and another in the ceiling are all that is required; the reflective tube connects the two and transmits light. Solatubes can be installed by anyone who has the skills required to install venting products through a roof; the company's one-piece flashing system allows water to bypass the tube without leakage. Solatube

makes both round and square units; accessories are available to overcome attic obstructions and other uncommon situations. The rooftop acrylic dome filters out all but 0.1 percent of incoming UV rays, and the ceiling diffuser filters out more than 96 percent of that, for a total UV filtering factor of 99.9 percent. Sun fading of carpets and other fabrics is nearly nonexistent.

Other innovations are also available. Solatube's Daylight Dimmer is a motorized baffle that mounts beneath the roof dome; a wall switch controls the baffle, making it possible to decrease the amount of light coming into the room, or to cut it off entirely. In areas where sunlight is not abundant, the company combines two technologies in its Brighten Up series of skylights to solve the problem. One, called an LITD (Light Intercepting Transfer Device), works in concert with the company's Raybender Fresnel lens to increase the amount of light capture at the roof dome level and deliver more light to the room below than would be possible with a simple skylight.

A more familiar approach is taken by Solar Innovations, whose traditional and modernist skylights

OPPOSITE: In spite of the custom appearance of this conservatory, it is designed around stock elements that can be combined in many different ways. The manufacturer has even designed a conservatory to be installed between two roof gables in a historic apartment house.

OPPOSITE, LEFT and RIGHT: Solatube skylights can be installed without the framing requirements of conventional skylights; their installation takes no more skill than putting in a roof vent. ABOVE, LEFT and RIGHT: Various models and sizes can meet the daylight requirements of any room, and the light can be modulated with an optional baffle.

are available in stock and custom configurations. Many of the company's designs are framed in aluminum, finished in a choice of five stock colors, clear or bronze anodized, or plain mill finish. Custom colors are also available. In addition, Solar Innovations offers mahogany framing that accents upscale designs perfectly. Stock shapes include barrel vaults, pyramids, ridge-mounted designs that hug a roof's peak, polygons, and a segmented dome that is greatly in demand for today's elaborate foyers with their extra ceiling height and curved stairs. Custom designs can be created by Solar Innovations's product specialists in collaboration with an architect. The company can produce nearly any shape needed, detailed in any style desired, using its modular elements. Solar Innovations can supply any of its designs with acrylic or polycarbonate plastic glazing, or with a choice of tempered or laminated safety glass. Glass is available in various tints and reflective versions that reduce heat load; different types can be combined in one design if necessary.

Solar Innovations also manufactures other glazing solutions, including curtain walls specifically made for houses. Curtain walls are the "glass walls" so beloved by modernist architects, but they've come a long way from the single-pane plate glass Frank Lloyd Wright used in his Pope-Leighey House in 1939. Twin-paned-glass technology has been around for some time, but only recently have improvements been made to the gaskets that hold the two panes in position with a space between them. Urethane gives gaskets much longer service life, so that twin-pane windows and curtain walls will not allow air to get between the panes, which creates condensation and compromises energy efficiency. Solar Innovations's curtain walls are made so that they can be used with the company's skylight components to create glazed structures such as entryways. The same range of finishes is available for curtain-wall framing as for skylights; the mill finish is particularly useful for retrofitting energy-efficient curtain walls into existing modernist houses, keeping the same look these houses had when new.

Other Solar Innovations prefab elements that can benefit homeowners are its conservatories and sunrooms. Both can be prefabricated to a homeowner's specifications; materials, color, glazing material, and detailing are similar in range to other products from the company. One of the more ornate traditional models recalls London's long-vanished Crystal Palace of 1851; others are more modern in appearance. Recently, Solar Innovations designed a conservatory to fit between two towers of a high-rise building, bringing a little nature into an urban environment.

OPPOSITE: Energy-efficient greenhouses, conservatories, window walls, and enclosures can all be custom-prefabricated to order by Solar Innovations. Modular elements in a wide variety of materials and finishes can be combined to create any desired look.

interior elements

ABOVE: Prefab kitchen cabinets avoid an overly repetitive look with variations in their doors. OPPOSITE: A bathroom appears to be highly customized, but is designed around a prefab shower pan and shower enclosure, as well as a prefab vanity. The cost savings help to make the tile affordable.

So much prefabrication is found in today's interiors that it goes largely unnoticed; it has become the way things are done, instead of an alternative to traditional methods. The trend has gone so far that some materials and finishes formerly taken for granted have been almost entirely replaced by prefab components. Ceramic tile was once found in the bathrooms of all but the very cheapest housing; now tile is a luxury material, supplanted in most new construction by a myriad of prefab showers and tubs in acrylic and fiberglass. Completely custom kitchen cabinets are not entirely unheard of, but they are extremely rare, and even they make use of prefab elements such as roll-out shelves. The great advantage of today's prefab interior elements is that there's a product for every taste and every purse. A great advantage is that many designs are banal, intended to please as many mass-market consumers as possible.

A few companies are bucking the trend, using prefabrication techniques to give consumers greater choice and more design flexibility. Two new ways to produce nearly unique prefab elements are CAD (Computer-Assisted Design) and CNC (Computer Numerically Controlled) cutting machinery. Formerly, parts of a prefabricated product had to be prototyped by hand; that

expense could be justified only when the design was to be mass-produced. Today, computers can be used to design every part of a prefab element, and CNC methods can produce very short runs of the design. Everything has been proven to fit together in the CAD drawings, eliminating the expensive prototype stage, and CNC cutting tools cost very little to program.

One company that takes full advantage of these methods is Adams Stair. Prefabricated stairs were once limited to a few utilitarian straight staircases and uninspired spiral designs. Adams Stair produces stairs in a wide variety of styles and finishes; the company's technology can produce nearly any stair an architect can dream up. Whether you'd like an Art Deco curved stair seemingly out of an Astaire and Rogers movie, a futuristic design, or a historically correct staircase for a restoration, the company can prefabricate it, ship it in unassembled or assembled form, and arrange for installation. Even the most demanding designs, such as the floating staircases seen in nineteenth-century mansions, can be prefabricated.

The company's secret is its CAD-controlled CNC lathes, capable of turning almost any of Adams's many stock baluster designs in two minutes. If something unusual is needed, such as a duplicate of a historic newel for a restoration, Adams can work with a homeowner or architect to come up with a CAD-designed copy, which is turned on the CNC lathe just as quickly as a stock element. Such flexibility used to come at a very high price; old lathes produced unique profiles by

means of a custom-made cutting knife that often cost several thousand dollars. Adams can produce the same result in most cases for a $125 programming fee. Once the CNC parts are produced, Adams can combine them with other stair parts to produce a final result that appears to be completely site-built.

OPPOSITE and ABOVE: Both the exquisite traditional stair at left, and the contemporary one seen above, were prefabricated by Adams Stair. OVERLEAF: The firm can supply any stair design in knocked-down form for on-site assembly, or a stair can be shipped assembled, to be dropped in place.

ABOVE and OPPOSITE: Focal Point's molding profiles can be combined in many different ways to produce effects as simple or as elaborate as required. The closed-cell polymer material cuts like white pine, and its finish requires no priming, reducing coats of paint that would obscure the detail.

Moldings are one of the touches that can make or break a house, particularly if historical accuracy is at stake. There's a great temptation to skimp; wood moldings are expensive to begin with, and many period rooms have details, such as crown moldings, that depend on combining several different components to create a single large-scale profile. Installation mistakes are easy to make, too: Every nail driven into wooden molding risks splitting the wood, and an inexperienced painter can obliterate delicate details with too much paint while trying to achieve good paint coverage. Focal Point Architectural Products makes moldings and architectural elements of closed-cell polymer that can go up with adhesive and screws or nails. Splitting concerns are minimized, since the polymer is consistent in density throughout, without weak spots. A surface finish eliminates priming, decreasing the amount of paint needed, and helping to ensure that Focal Point's crisp detail is maintained. Joints between sections are filled with vinyl-based spackle. The polymer is the same density as white pine, and can be cut and worked with the same tools as wood.

Focal Point makes moldings, niches, ceiling domes and medallions, panel moldings, window and door casings, and stair brackets. Some classical details traditionally rendered in plaster, such as rosettes and friezes (carved decorative elements seen just below a crown molding), are also available. The company's FocalFlex and Contour-All products are capable of conforming to curved surfaces, such as the walls of an

OPPOSITE, LEFT and RIGHT: Focal Point products can be used nearly anywhere; their polymer construction is dimensionally stable and moisture-resistant. ABOVE, LEFT and RIGHT: Requirements for support construction are greatly reduced when compared to traditional, heavy wood and plaster elements, lowering project costs and minimizing construction time.

oval foyer. For period architecture, Focal Point makes moldings and other details authorized by the Colonial Williamsburg Foundation and several other historical associations. If a more modern look is desired, Focal Point's Frank Lloyd Wright Collection offers friezes based on Wright's organic motifs.

Homeowners who are interested in marble or stone counters in kitchen or bath quickly find that these materials are much harder to select and install than laminates or solid surfacing materials such as Corian. Many stone counters are custom fabricated by local stone companies, to the measure of the builder, contractor, or homeowner. Those wanting to put their stone-counter installation on a faster track can take advantage of prefab stone counters from Global Stone Company. Colored marbles, onyx, travertine, granite, and slate are all offered. The company has a sample-loan program to help assure that consumers get exactly the color and veining they want. Sink cut-outs and other installation-specific details can be cut in a stock section by Global Stone before a counter is shipped to the consumer. Installation is much the same as for solid surfacing materials; the company offers a line of installation accessories. One of the advantages of prefab stone is that working with standard sections eliminates the "you measured it, you bought it" problem inherent in custom-cut stone.

LEFT: Stone countertops are now prefabricated; available in stock shapes that can be combined to create any design needed. Variations in stone, edge profile, and thickness are all available; measuring, special ordering, and extended waits for delivery are eliminated.

ABOVE, LEFT and RIGHT: Polyester solid-surface countertop materials such as Corian have come a long way since their bland, beige days. Up-to-date sink profiles give a more contemporary look than older designs. OPPOSITE: More realistic stone looks and intense color are now available as well.

Many builders and architects making extensive use of prefab elements resort to traditional wall finishes such as Sheetrock inside their houses. Although Sheetrock is versatile and almost universally acceptable to homeowners, it does require considerable hand finishing, plus painting or wallpapering. A one-step approach to interior walls is available from Homasote; the company makes several products it terms "tackable" wall panels. Homasote panels are made from the company's mainstay product, a board molded from post-consumer (recycled) paper fiber. Available in several fire ratings, Homasote products are both "green" and convenient. DesignWall is a fabric-covered four-by-eight-foot panel with a surface that looks like homespun cloth; a wide range of colors is offered. Since DesignWall is both a substrate and a surface finish, installation consists of little more than nailing it directly to the wall studs in a house. The fabric's texture can conceal where the panel is nailed, or battens (narrow strips of wood) can be used between panels to cover the nailing edge. If more wall texture is desired, Homasote makes a panel that is installed the same way as DesignWalls, but is finished in burlap instead. In addition to the advantages of the one-step installation process, Homasote's wall panels add additional R-value to a house's insulation.

One of Homasote's newest products is a boon for any family with members whose activities make noise. For children's rooms, media rooms, and other locations where sound control is needed, Homasote also makes 440 SoundBarrier, a structural board available in several

versions intended for use as walls, floor underlayment, or ceilings. Several panel sizes are available; smaller panels are easier to handle for ceiling installations. 440 SoundBarrier can be used as a substrate underneath conventional Sheetrock, or a fabric-covered version can be special ordered, to give the same "tackable" advantages as DesignWalls, plus sound deadening. ■

OPPOSITE: The luxurious countertop shown here can be achieved in prefab stone, or in solid-surface polyester materials. ABOVE: One advantage of the synthetic is that it can be repaired almost invisibly if chipped or burned; gloss can be restored on-site by buffing.

roofs

SIPs are an excellent choice for roof panels, but as with any roof, finish roofing must be applied. Conventional roofing materials have always been problematic. On pitched (sloped) roofs, shingles are tedious and expensive to install, and can easily be loosened by wind action or by freeze/thaw cycles in winter. When a shingled roof wears out, it is not usually advisable to re-roof over the existing shingles with more of the same; the deteriorated old shingles are not a good substrate for new ones. Ripping off the old shingles is costly and messy, and the environmental impact of the debris is high.

Conventional materials used for flat roofs are even more of a problem; they consist of tar spread in a layer on the roof, with gravel as a protective surface. Tar is environmentally unfriendly, and its application often fails; a tiny gap in the tar that goes unnoticed during installation can create leakage problems that are very difficult to pinpoint, particularly since the tar is covered with gravel, by the time leaks occur. Flat roofs are also susceptible to ponding, a situation where water collects in any spot slightly lower than its surroundings. If a gap in the tar occurs where the roof is likely to pond, a nightmarish situation all too familiar to owners of modernist houses and commercial structures results. Even very modest rains can leak through a roof with these problems.

Fortunately, new products are available that decrease environmental impact, ease installation, and resist leakage. One of the biggest strides forward has been made with flat roofs, formerly so routinely problematic that many architects would not design them. Duro-Last Roofing's single-ply membrane system makes flat and very low-slope roofs practical; the product is made of a thermoplastic sheet bonded to a knitted-fabric scrim. A Duro-Last roof is fabricated to order in the company's factory, with most necessary seaming done under highly controlled conditions. The installation process is somewhat akin to making a bed with a contour sheet; the membrane is smoothed into place over the roof, and then over its edges. Attachment can be handled by a mechanical system of retaining bars at roof edges, or the membrane can

OPPOSITE, LEFT and RIGHT: A Duro-Last roofing membrane is easy to apply to a flat roof; the process is somewhat akin to stretching a contour sheet onto a bed. Special retaining members secure the edges. For tricky installations, the product can be cut and seamed on-site.

be fully adhered to the roof. The membrane can be formed to accommodate elements such as plumbing vents; it extends up the side of the vent, and is secured to it with stainless-steel banding.

Duro-Last is suited to both new and existing roofs. Its quick and easy installation has made the product a favorite in San Francisco's Bay Area, home to a significant concentration of modernist houses with low-slope roofs. The houses are known affectionately as "Eichlers," after visionary builder Joseph Eichler, who was inspired to build them as affordable modernism when he lived in a Frank Lloyd Wright house. Eichler owners appreciate the minimal disruption of a Duro-Last installation; the appearance of the white membrane is similar to the white gravel used on the houses originally. Since Eichlers are of post-and-beam construction, with a very thin roof structure, high resistance to leakage is important; water intrusion drips directly into a room as soon as it begins. Duro-Last's membrane

prefab elements

has proved highly beneficial to Eichler owners, whose famous, highly sought-after houses are a valuable investment that must be protected.

For roofs with a greater slope, known as pitched roofs, Tallant Industries's Ondura roofing sheets are a choice that makes it possible to have an attractive, highly water-resistant roof that can be installed quickly by anyone with average do-it-yourself skills. Made of asphalt-impregnated fiber, the sheets come in a corrugated version that measures 48 inches by 79 inches, or a Spanish tile–look version that measures 48 inches by 19½ inches. The sheets are lightweight and easy to handle; even the larger corrugated ones weigh only 18 pounds each. The material is easy to cut with regular saws, and cut edges are not sharp, minimizing the risk of injury during installation. Available in gray, black, white, green, blue, red, brown, and tan, Ondura roofs have an attractive appearance when installed. The product is paintable if none of the eight standard colors are suitable for a given house.

Ondura has environmental benefits as well; it can be installed over an existing shingled roof without any need to remove old shingles whose toxic components might leach into a landfill. Wood strips called purlins are nailed over the old shingles, and the Ondura sheets are then nailed to the purlins with Ondura's special nails, which attach the sheets firmly. Since the new roof does not touch the old, the Ondura installation is not vulnerable to failure due to problems with the existing shingles. Roof ridges are finished with ridge caps made of the same material as the sheets; Ondura makes a ridge ventilation product called Ridgeline that can be installed under ridge caps to permit hot air to rise from an attic. Ondura is compatible with conventional metal flashing where the roof meets side walls or changes slope, and the company makes a pipe-flashing accessory in two sizes to handle flashing of plumbing and other vents.

Ondura can also be used as wall siding; wall installations are even easier than roofs. Tallant also makes a roofing sheet called Tuftex that can be nailed directly to the rafters of outdoor living and utility areas with no need for roof decking. Available in several colors and translucent or clear, Tuftex comes in three different materials to suit the needs of various projects. The most versatile is Tuftex's PolyCarbonate material, an extremely durable plastic that comes in a crystal-clear version ideally suited to sunrooms. Although Tuftex is not intended to be used as a primary roof on a house or commercial building, its light weight and high strength make it an excellent choice for other roofs. ▪

OPPOSITE: Prefabricated sheet roofing goes on easily and quickly, but metal types are not suited for most residential styles. Ondura's asphalt-impregnated fiber is lightweight, installs with common tools, and yields a tile-like look suitable for most houses.

prefab room **additions**

Once limited strictly to conventional construction that was closely matched to an existing house, room additions have gone prefab, too. Although prefab additions can be abutted against a house, or linked by a passageway, some homeowners are electing to build freestanding additions. The idea has several advantages: Privacy is enforced by even a small distance from a main house, a big advantage for offices and guesthouses. Aural privacy is greater, too: A family member wanting to crank up a home theater system to its limits can do so in a detached, sound-proofed media room without disturbing others. And many of the rigors of remodeling can be avoided, since the main house does not have to be altered.

Additions that are semidetached or detached have one other advantage: Since they are visually separate from the house they serve, they do not have to

match it. The rigors of locating windows, brick or siding, roofing, and trim that match those elements on the existing house can be almost completely eliminated. All that is necessary is an appreciation for scale, and an avoidance of materials that clash with, or imitate, those found in the main house. We've gotten beyond the "matchy-matchy" in our wardrobes and our furnishings; eliminating it from our architecture would seem to be a logical next step.

One of the most promising prefab approaches to additions is from the Austrian architect Oskar Leo Kaufmann, who has invented a panelized prefab system he has dubbed OA.SYS, for Open Architecture System. OA.SYS is a collection of modular panels that can be combined with nearly complete freedom to create any house or addition required. Modernist in style, completed OA.SYS buildings are uniformly high in architectural quality; Kaufmann has seen to it that the proportions of each panel in the system is sympathetic in scale to every other, no matter which is juxtaposed with which.

Some panels are solid wall units, some are punctuated with windows and doors of varying sizes, and some are almost entirely glass. The structural strength is high; Kaufmann's clients are requesting—

OPPOSITE: Austrian architect Oskar Leo Kaufmann has devised the OA.SYS system of prefab building elements that can be combined to form complete houses. Panels with doors and windows are mixed with blank panels to create a high standard of modernist design at low cost.

LEFT: The OA.SYS method of building includes an interior finish system; walls can be either plywood or drywall. Wiring and other utilities such as telephone and Internet cabling are pre-installed. ABOVE: Windows are twin-paned, and upgrades are available for many system features.

putting it together

prefab elements

and getting—two- and even three-story designs. The panels can be ordered with customized variations, so that complete individuality results. There is even a Kaufmann structure available that is ready to install with no assembly required, the FRED room unit. The FRED is rectangular when installed but telescopes into a more compact cube for shipping. When a FRED is delivered, it has only to be placed on a slab and connected to utilities; a motorized electronic system expands it into its final shape. The FRED is particularly suited to guesthouse and office applications, since its amenities include a toilet. The large glass area of the front admits plenty of daylight to the interior. Like all of Kaufmann's products, FRED is well insulated, able to deliver energy-efficient living.

A self-contained approach is also taken by the designer Edgar Blazona in his Modular Dwellings, complete, ready-to-assemble prefab rooms that include everything, even interior finish and foundations. Blazona's rooms are modernist, glass-fronted structures. Though they're not stylistically suited to the backyard of every house, they are some of the most architecturally significant prefab structures in existence.

Blazona's MD 120 room measures 10 feet by 12, and is steel framed, with both glass and hardwood on its exterior. Modular Dwellings are designed to be assembled by the owner on Pin Foundation's Diamond Pier pin-foundation system, so the MD 120 is easily and quickly installed. The MD 120 can be disassembled

OPPOSITE: FRED is an Oskar Leo Kaufmann design that almost installs itself; the two sections of the one-room unit telescope courtesy of an electronically controlled motor. ABOVE: Placement on a concrete slab and connection to utilities are the only other steps needed to put FRED to work.

LEFT and ABOVE: Edgar Blazona's Modular Dwellings bring affordability back to modernist design. The lightweight structures make excellent freestanding room additions and vacation cabins. They're suitable for installation using the Diamond Pier pin-foundation system shown in Chapter 2.

and moved to another location. Another model, the MD 42, was designed in collaboration with Brice Gamble; at 6 by 8 feet, it's compact enough to be transported almost fully assembled, yet has room for a pull-out bed that's included in its price. At the room's destination, the windows can be put in place and the structure readied for use very quickly.

For a freestanding guest room, Blazona's MD 144 is generously sized at 12 feet by 12, with one translucent fiberglass wall in addition to its glass front. A sleeping loft is part of the design, so none of the room's floor space is encumbered by a bed. For those who don't feel the prefab approach is right for them, the designer offers a set of plans for the MD 100, a room similar to the MD 120, but wood framed, buildable at a tenth the price of Blazona's ready-built structures. And the MD 100's plans allow for do-it-yourself prefabrication; the room's parts can be built in one place and assembled in another.

All of Edgar Blazona's prefab rooms are modernism at its most—ahem—traditional; his designs are highly, deliberately reminiscent of Charles Eames and Richard Neutra houses. His goal is to make modernism affordable again; he is currently working on entire houses. The first, completed in 2004, was designed to be sold in a manner as modern as its look, in an auction on eBay. Whether that concept proves workable or not, Blazona's rooms and houses are something that have not been available for a long time: modernist architecture the average person can own.

OPPOSITE and **ABOVE**: Modular Dwellings come in a variety of configurations, and can be disassembled and re-erected if required. Designer Edgar Blazona is developing an entire house using the same techniques seen in his one-room structures; it's intended to revive the mid-century ethic of low-cost modernism.

Geodesic domes, pioneered by the Dymaxion House inventor Buckminster Fuller, have been around awhile. Early domes were susceptible to leakage, and required special windows and doors. Faze Change Produx has refined the concept in ways that make it more flexible and affordable than in Fuller's day and introduced the Econ-O-Dome. Faze Change Produx's founder, Wil Fidroeff, was a friend of the Fuller family after Buckminster Fuller's death and learned many nuances of geodesic construction as a result. In recent years, he has invented a few more.

Econ-O-Dome's geodesic structures differ from other manufacturers' in one major way: Fidroeff has found ways to interrupt the dome's 120-degree panel geometry, allowing for large, flat vertical surfaces, suitable for the insertion of standard doors and windows. The concept also makes it easier to link domes with each other, by abutting them, and with existing structures, through the use of simple, enclosed passageways. Econ-O-Domes are available as simple frame kits

OPPOSITE: When invented by Buckminster Fuller, geodesic domes required great skill to design and erect. Today, prefabricated dome kits make domes a do-it-yourself project. Fuller's basic concept has been greatly refined over the years; it is now possible to insert doors into the geometry of a dome without resorting to a separate entryway, as was once necessary. Elastomeric paints form an outer skin for today's domes, so there's no longer a need to shingle the entire structure.

and as frames with precut outer panels of cement-fiber board. Interiors can be finished conventionally with Sheetrock, or interior panels may be ordered—precut, they are of gypsum board backed with rigid foam insulation. Additionally, frames designed for heavy snow loads are offered, and a "designer" frame kit is offered that is attractive when exposed in a dome's interior.

Fidroeff's customers back up his assertion that domes are easy for owners to build: "We put the ten prefab trapezoids above the riser wall in about an hour. The rest of the dome frame was assembled in about a day," says one. Weatherproofing is often a bugbear in dome construction, with many domes being conventionally shingled. Econ-O-Dome recommends an elastomeric paint finish over the cement-fiber outer panels, which are already highly weather-resistant. Seams at panel edges are handled with what Fidroeff terms a "saturated seal," a woven polyester tape saturated with the same elastomeric paint used on the rest of the exterior. Not only is the appearance of the completed dome a stronger architectural statement than a dome with shingles, but leaks are easily dealt with by painting on more elastomeric. Econ-O-Dome offers custom-design services, and plans for those wanting to build from scratch.

You *can* have a custom house, exactly the way you've always dreamed it would be. Thinking of prefab elements as building blocks, infinitely variable in their arrangement, is the way your ideas can take on real shape and form with amazing speed, giving you your house, your way, right now.

CHAPTER 3

using prefab elements

homes on the **cutting edge**

Using prefab elements is much simpler today than in the past. Formerly the exclusive province of professionals, building in general is now a much more transparent process. Because of the enormous do-it-yourself market, prefab manufacturers have become especially sensitive to the needs of consumers. It was once enough to manufacture a component; today, information, service, technical support, and installation are all consumer demands that must be addressed.

Consumers and home buyers who were once content to select wallpaper, paint, and flooring now possess a great deal of "armchair expertise," thanks to such TV shows as *This Old House* and Bob Vila's *Home Again*. People who once knew nothing about, say, their heating system aside from the fact that it was in the basement have now seen a range of systems discussed, installed, and repaired, with quite a lot of attention to detail. The same is true of every system in a house; today's consumer generally has a very fair idea of what products are available, what they do, and how they are supposed to be installed. Armchair expertise is no substitute for professional experience, but homeowners and home buyers today are not completely at the mercy of a builder or contractor, as was true for most of the last century

The biggest change in prefab elements is, of course, the service level made possible by the Internet. Almost every manufacturer has a Web site, and even the least informative ones give more information than consumers got in the old "trust me" days. Instead of poring over magazines, writing to P.O. Box addresses, and getting back skimpy brochures, consumers now have direct access to the same information their architect, builder, or contractor will have. The benefits are enormous: Many a poor choice can be averted immediately, before a prefab element is ordered or an expensive professional's time wasted, and the smallest details of operation or maintenance can be known in advance. Although much of the information on manufacturers' home pages is the same old "features, advantages, and benefits" ad-speak everyone is familiar with, delving deeper into Web sites pays huge dividends.

Some of the information to be found on manufacturers' Web sites includes:

- Exact dimensions and weights.

- Detailed technical information, including composition of materials used in the product, horsepower or other ratings of motors, temperature ranges in which the product is designed to perform, and information on energy consumption.

- Installation information, often complete with recommended materials and tools, safety requirements, and limitations, such as situations in which the product should not be used.

- Complete operating manuals.

- Warranty information, including limitations and exclusions in the warranty.

- Results of tests or studies that substantiate performance claims.

- Technical drawings, often in AutoCAD format, that can be cut and pasted into working drawings, eliminating possibility of dimensional errors.

Focal Point molded architectural elements.

Consumers surfing the Internet for information on prefab elements should be sure that they have two basic tools on their computers: Adobe Acrobat Reader and Autodesk DWF Viewer.

Adobe Acrobat Reader is often needed for viewing installation instructions, operating manuals, and the like; it uses a format called PDF (portable document file). PDF files found on Web sites can be saved. In Windows operating systems or in Macintosh operating systems, all that is necessary is to right-click on the link to the file and select "Save Target As" or "Download Link to Disk." The PDF document can then be opened on the hard drive, or even e-mailed to someone else needing the information. PDF documents cannot be edited with Acrobat Reader, only viewed. If you don't have Acrobat Reader, a visit to www.adobe.com will allow you to download it, free.

AutoCAD drawings are becoming more and more common on manufacturer Web sites, because they are detailed CAD (Computer-Assisted Design) drawings of a product, accurate to the last detail. Most architects today design projects in AutoCAD, or in a similar product using the same file formats. They can pick up a CAD drawing of a prefab element from the Internet and insert it into plans quickly, with the assurance that the element will fit into the project exactly as intended. A consumer researching prefab elements online can also make use of AutoCAD drawings. Using the Autodesk DWF Viewer, consumers can look at CAD drawings to gain greater understanding of an element, or for help in deciding if suggesting it to their

architect, builder, or contractor is appropriate. Autodesk DWF Viewer does not allow changes or markings to be made on an AutoCAD drawing; like Adobe Acrobat Reader, it is strictly a viewer. For those who want to mark possible changes on a plan without changing the plan itself, Autodesk DWF Composer is an excellent tool and does not require a huge learning curve.

For more ambitious consumers, it is possible to use AutoCAD drawings in home-generated plans, and even to exchange plan drawings with others, such as those made by an architect. Although CAD software requires some time and training to use, it has many advantages for anyone making the necessary investment. If a homeowner wants to explore the possibility of moving a wall shown on an architect's drawing, CAD software makes it possible to make the change right on the original drawing. The resulting CAD file can be e-mailed to the architect, allowing her or him to see exactly what is desired, rather than relying on guesswork or an interpretation of a verbal description. It should, however, be borne in mind that moving a line and relocating an actual design element are two very different things; an architect's experience may well indicate that the change a client wants is very expensive, or even impossible, to accomplish. CAD software can improve communication, but it is no substitute for the judgment of a professional.

Although AutoCAD is expensive, professional-quality software, what might be termed "clones" are much more affordable and available to consumers. These do not necessarily have all the features of AutoCAD itself, but they use the same DWF and DWG file formats, so they can be used to mark, change, and exchange AutoCAD files. Some of the better-known "clones," as well as AutoCAD itself, are described in the next chapter, along with information on software manufacturers' Web sites and purchase information.

warranties

The warranties that are offered with the purchase of many prefab elements are a godsend to today's consumers. Not only can they offer significant protection to the owner while the product is in use, many can help when it's time to sell. Most buyers and lenders demand a warranty on certain systems of a house; sometimes even a "wall-to-wall" warranty is required for a limited period of time. If prefab elements have been used in a house's construction, their warranties may help meet these requirements.

The protection of a warranty should be factored into the decision-making process when the purchase of a prefab element is being considered. Obviously, length of protection is important, but other questions should get satisfactory answers before a prefab element is selected:

■ Get a written copy of the warranty before committing to any major purchase. It's strongly recommended that consumers obtain a printed copy from the manufacturer by mail, instead of downloading a copy from the Internet. A downloaded copy may not be the latest revision; many Web sites contain some outdated material.

■ Beware of the term "Lifetime Guarantee," which can mean the consumer's lifetime, the usual life expectancy of the product, or the lifetime of the owner's ownership of the house in which the element is installed.

■ Is the warranty transferable? A transferable warranty can be a big selling point for a house, and it can relieve a seller of responsibility for that particular element if the house must be warranted when it is sold.

■ Many elements require professional installation; the *kind* of installer may make an enormous difference in the event of a warranty claim. The three most common arrangements are:

1. **Owner-selected professional installers.** A manufacturer may offer labor coverage for installations performed by such installers, or may not. If coverage is offered, it's often limited to labor needed to remove and reinstall the part in the event of failure; the installation itself is not guaranteed.

2. **Manufacturer-recommended installers.** Many manufacturers are happy to refer owners to local installers. Use of such an installer will sometimes result in labor coverage, but there are exceptions. The time to find out whether or not use of the recommended installer will increase warranty coverage is before you decide to purchase. If you're

told that such use will result in a labor warranty, get it in writing before you commit to purchase.

3. **Manufacturer-authorized installers.** These are local companies that a manufacturer has a relationship with, and they are generally the best bet for maximum warranty coverage. The manufacturer very often trains such installers, and the company has a vested interest in maintaining a high standard of installation, since consistently substandard work can result in the loss of a valuable contract or relationship. Usually, products that have this kind of installation available are also purchased through the local company performing the installation.

■ Does the warranty exclude damage caused by the product's failure? For instance, a leaking roof or window can damage roof deck, ceiling, wall, subfloor, and finish floor materials. Some states do not allow warranties to exclude such damages, but many do.

■ If related damages are included, are they limited to failure of the product only, or are failures related to installation also included? The best bet for obtaining coverage for labor-related failures is to select a product whose purchase includes manufacturer-authorized installation.

■ Never take a salesperson's word for warranty coverage of any kind. If the coverage is not spelled out in a printed warranty or in a contract, it does not legally exist in most instances. If written coverage is not available, or if a salesperson seemingly can't be pinned down on the issue, look elsewhere.

prefab elements and building codes

Most of the possible code problems with prefab elements stem from their misuse, not from the elements themselves. The exception is complete prefab structures, which sometimes have local code restrictions preventing their use or making some modification necessary.

Meeting code requirements is so complex that it really should be left to an architect or an experienced builder if an entire house is being built. Mistakes can be made at every step of the process, from plans to final inspection, and they can be costly to correct. Regarding prefab elements to a repair or remodeling job, it's sometimes possible for the layman to get through the code maze unaided, but don't count on it unless the scope of the job is quite small, such as replacing windows or finishing roofing.

In general, at least two codes will apply in your locality. They will vary according to the location of the project; the United States does not have a uniform building code. Your state will have its codes, and your municipality probably will, too, although some municipalities do not have codes of their own, relying on the state code instead. Your state will usually have a state building code office or a state bookstore where the state code can be purchased. If you're unable to find such a resource, try contacting a local code inspector to find out where copies are available. For most states, and for many major municipalities, Contractor-Books.com, at http://www.contractor-books.com/Bldg_Codes.htm#States has code books available for purchase.

If you are determined to research codes and draw plans yourself, it's a very good idea to request an appointment to meet with a building inspector before you begin to design. The building inspector can guide you past common pitfalls in the code, and the two of you can establish a working relationship. You should ask questions and listen to answers in a courteous, professional manner, rather than commenting on the difficulties presented by the code, because most inspectors interpret such comments as a signal that the job will need to be closely monitored. An inspector whose suspicions have been aroused can choose to inspect very closely indeed. For this reason, builders and architects work very hard at maintaining good relationships with code compliance officials.

Your inspector may want to see your plans at an early stage, before all possible details are fleshed out. This is a favor to you, to see if your basic plan (floor plan and elevations) meets code before you waste any time on other details that can't be used because the basic plan was not compliant. The inspector may even want to check several times at several different stages. The better you comply in the early stages, the easier things will be later. Inspectors have the power to deny you a building permit, and they can deny you a certificate of occupancy until the job is completed to their satisfaction, so staying on good, professional terms with them is essential.

Some prefab elements may be unfamiliar to the building inspector. Since it is easier to say "No" than it is to do research, many inspectors will withhold approval if they have not seen something before. The way around this is to do the inspector's research for him or her. You should have complete information on the elements you want to use, and it should be ready for the inspector to look at when you're discussing plans. Drawings, specifications, and installation guides should all be obtained from an element's manufacturer, to help the inspector understand if the element is admissible under applicable codes. If you're told it does not meet code, ask if there's anything in the inspector's discretionary powers that will permit him or her to consider the element for approval. There is often an "Alternative Systems and Materials" section in the code for just this purpose; if something new comes along that is better than the code requires, the inspector may consider it. Many manufacturers who have an unusual product have had extensive testing or studies performed to substantiate their claims of product performance. If such results are available, you should have them available for the inspector to look at when you present your request.

Although the most extensive homework won't guarantee that your proposed element will be acceptable, most inspectors will be much more favorably disposed to considering alternative methods if you've been professional enough to gather the information needed to help them decide. ▪

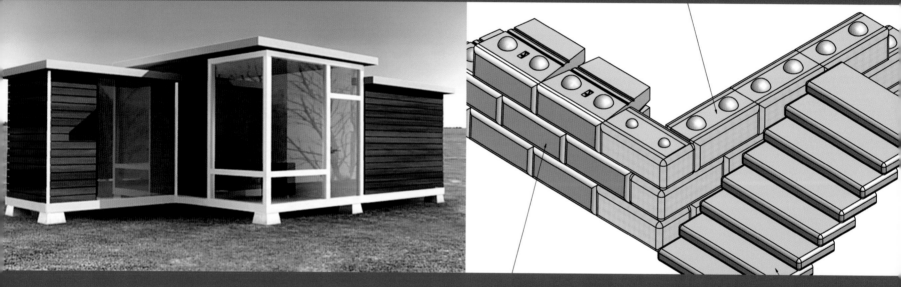

puter-assisted design

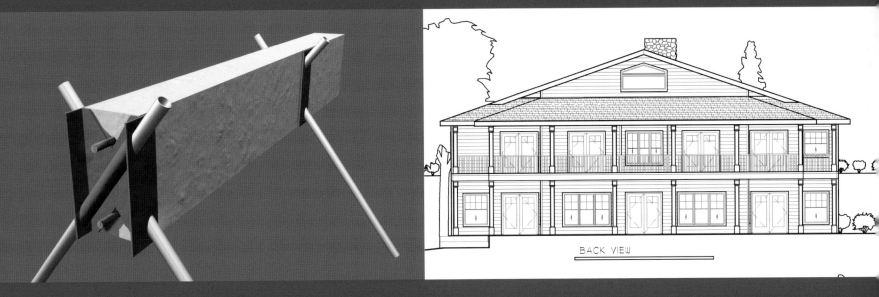

BACK VIEW

tools you can use

Anyone who is building will almost certainly be working with an architect to realize his or her goals for a new house. Though it's certainly possible for an owner to conceive of a floor plan and to draw it, hiring an architect is the only way for most owners to obtain all the services necessary to turn a plan into reality. Architects are experienced in working with building-code requirements and can muster engineering resources for tricky projects. Architect-drawn plans generally pass building-permit approvals the first time, saving headaches and money. And an architect has a reservoir of experience that helps him or her guide clients around pitfalls that will make an enormous difference in a house's livability. Most of us cannot tell from a plan that a small bathroom might be claustrophobic. An architect can usually spot such problems right away.

If you're hoping to make extensive use of prefab elements in a new house, you should find out how the architect feels about what you're interested in. If the architect is not enthusiastic about extensive use of prefab elements in general, you may want to shop for another architect. If they have an objection to one or two of the particular elements you present for their consideration, it's a good idea to consider it carefully. Architects may know that local builders are incapable of working with it, or that there's a local code problem, or they may have used it before, and found that it didn't live up to its advertising claims. They may also know of something much more workable for your particular house.

As helpful as architects can be, using prefab elements effectively and creatively in plans for rebuilding and remodeling is no longer their exclusive province. Thanks to today's CAD (Computer-Assisted Design) software, it is easy to grab plan material for a prefab component from the Internet, then drag and drop it into CAD-designed plans, whether drawn by the architect or by you. You can see, easily and cheaply, if a particular idea or product is going to work or not. If you're working with an architect, this doesn't bypass his or her skills; it allows you to try ideas before you're on the architect's time, presenting him or her with only the few that seem feasible. That allows an architect to work quickly, because you've identified what seems to suit your needs, and you've already determined that it should fit the plan. One caveat: Your architect knows many things you don't, for instance knowing that putting a tub on one bathroom wall instead of another could add $1,500 to the job in additional plumbing costs. Don't be afraid to present your ideas, but trust the professional who is trying to help you. And if having things your way is more important to you than taking an architect's advice, be prepared to pay the added cost.

The CAD product used by most design professionals is AutoCAD. It is extremely versatile, but too costly for most homeowners to purchase for use on the occasional project. Fortunately, consumer-oriented clones of AutoCAD are much less expensive than the original and they can read and export files in AutoCAD's special DWF format. Although not all of AutoCAD's features can be found in the clones, they do make it possible to draw, read, change, and e-mail drawings; consumers can now exchange ideas with an architect

CAD techologies enabled Topsider Homes to focus on one-of-a-kind custom-designed structures.

many miles away, via the Internet, in the form of plans the architect can easily understand.

CAD software has become easier to use in recent years, but it's a good idea to be patient, use the tutorial provided, and expect to take a while to become proficient enough to become creative. For AutoCAD itself, online tutorials are available, as well as classes in most community colleges and universities. The online tutorials for AutoCAD can be useful to purchasers of other CAD software, since many are designed to work and feel as much like AutoCAD as possible. If the clone you select baffles you a bit, get on the Internet and look for AutoCAD tutorials; you'll soon understand more about your clone. Clone-specific tutorials are available in some instances; Google the name of your clone to see what's being offered.

Even if a consumer wants to leave all the drawing of plans to an architect, it's often useful to be able to open AutoCAD files found on the Web sites of manufacturers. AutoCAD has a free downloadable viewer available its Web site, listed in the Software Sources section below. A viewer allows you to look at files, but not to make changes to them, such as dropping a manufacturer's drawings into a plan. To do that, you'll need to get one of the clones.

Here is a selection of some of the software that will make it easier for you to use prefab elements. Be certain to check the system requirements of any software before purchasing, to be sure that your computer has the minimum operating system, hard drive space, and memory needed to run the program. Not all CAD pro-

grams are available in a version for Macintosh systems; check software manufacturer Web sites listed in the Software Sources section below for more information.

software sources

From AutoCAD:

AutoCAD 2005 This is what your architect uses, and though it's expensive, it can create drawings for any project you can imagine. Three-dimensional rendering is possible, as are photorealistic presentation drawings showing exactly what a completed project will look like. Extensive training is necessary to use AutoCAD, but its capabilities are almost boundless. Under $4,000; available at the Autodesk Online Store at www.autodesk.com.

Autodesk DWF Composer For those who need both a viewer and the ability to mark desired changes on a plan, this is an inexpensive way to accomplish the job. Marking changes is not the same as making changes to the plan itself, but it's an easy way to show an architect what you have in mind. Available at the Autodesk Online Store at www.autodesk.com. Under $100.

Autodesk DWF Viewer From the AutoCAD people, this viewer makes it possible to look at any AutoCAD file you download from a manufacturer's Web site. Available for free download at www.autodesk.com.

Other Helpful Software:

CADopia IntelliCAD Standard Edition 4 This software is capable of importing AutoCAD files, permitting the user to work with them, and permitting the changed file to be sent back to an AutoCAD user. Many commands are the same as those used in AutoCAD, so migration to this clone is easy for those who already know how to use AutoCAD. Under $150 at the CADopia eStore; go to www.cadopia.com, and click on the eStore link.

CADopia IntelliCAD Professional Edition 4 This edition has the same capabilities as IntelliCAD Standard, plus photorealistic 3-D modeling for presentation drawings. Under $350 at the CADopia eStore; go to www.cadopia.com, and click on the eStore link.

CADopia IntelliCAD Rhino This plug-in allows animation of 3-D modeling done with IntelliCAD Professional Edition. Available bundled with CADopia IntelliCAD Professional Edition, above, and CADopia IntelliCAD Flamingo, below. Under $1,000 at the CADopia eStore; go to www.cadopia.com, and click on the eStore link.

CADopia IntelliCAD Flamingo Another IntelliCAD plug-in, this one permits animated "walk-by," "drive-by," even "fly-by" views of a project, making it possible to experience a project before it is built. Available bundled with CADopia IntelliCAD Professional Edition and CADopia IntelliCAD Rhino, above. Under $1,000 at the CADopia eStore; go to www.cadopia.com, and click on the eStore link.

F.I.T. CADVANCE 6.5 FIT stands for Furukawa Information Technology, a company making CAD software competitive with AutoCAD. Version 6.5 is an older version of CADVANCE that is available for free download from the FIT site at http://www.cadvance.com/index.html. Newer versions are available; they are competitively priced with AutoCAD products, starting at $1,995 for CADVANCE Version 2002. The older version is free for the downloading because FIT is committed to making CAD software available to anyone who needs it, as a public service. If you can do without today's bells and whistles, Version 6.5 can be very useful. It runs on Windows 3.1, as well as Windows versions 95 and higher.

KeyCAD PRO For basic 2-D plan drawing and for creating elevations, neither the functionality nor the price of this program can be beat. It has been discontinued by its manufacturer, Softkey Incorporated, but some software Web sites still have it available. KeyCAD PRO has two major limitations: Its proprietary KEY file format cannot be read by other CAD programs, and it cannot read AutoCAD formats such as DWG and DWF. But for making a readable, accurately scaled plan without the learning curve other CAD software requires, there's nothing like it. Usually under $30; go to www.google.com and search on "keycad" to find online vendors who still have stock.

glossary

Although most of the terms used in this book will be familiar to anyone who has built or remodeled a house before, first-timers may want to look in the following glossary for definitions. If a definition includes a word in uppercase, the definition of that word is also to be found here.

ACRYLIC: A plastic long familiar in its clear formulation as Plexiglas, acrylic is now produced in a range of colors. High in strength, resistant to impact.

AutoCAD: The leading brand of CAD software, considered the industry standard for most design projects, although some competing brands are compatible with its file format. See entry for CAD.

BALUSTER: The spindles that support the handrail of a stair along its length. The ends of the rail are supported by NEWELS.

CAD: Computer-Assisted Design. Sophisticated computer software that permits designs to be drawn, rendered in three dimensions, rotated for different views, and checked for fit against other designs.

CANTILEVER: An ELEMENT projecting from a house or building, supported only where it joins the structure. Balconies are the most common use of cantilevering. If a CORBEL is helping to support an ELEMENT, the element is not truly cantilevered.

CHASE: A recess in a wall, ceiling, or floor structure that accommodates the passage of pipes, wires, etc. Nearly always concealed behind a surface finish.

CNC: Computer Numerically Controlled. Cutting or machining technology that is controlled by computer programming, yielding a highly precise result capable of being reproduced endlessly. CNC machinery is usually programmed with CAD software.

CODE: A set of regulations governing the standards to which a structure must be built in a given locality; codes vary according to local requirements, geographic conditions, and customs.

CORBEL: An ELEMENT that projects from a wall, to support a structure extending from the wall. Corbels often support bay windows and balconies.

CURTAIN WALL: A section of exterior wall that does not bear weight, the load is borne by columns alongside a curtain wall's span. Curtain walls can be glass, or of other materials.

ELASTOMERIC PAINT: A paint formulated to remain rubbery in consistency after curing, designed to flex with the surface to which it has been applied.

ELEMENT: A part used in building a house; may be visible or not, and may be structural or decorative.

FENESTRATION: The arrangement or design of windows in a house.

FINISH ROOFING: The visible external surface of a roof; may be made of almost any water-resistant material.

FOUNDATION: The supporting structure on which a house rests, most often of masonry or stone construction.

GEODESIC DOME: A dome composed of triangular panels, or glazing ELEMENTS held in triangular frames.

GLAZING: Transparent or translucent ELEMENTS that admit light into a house. May be fixed, or may be made to open for ventilation.

GREEN: Describes materials that are designed and manufactured with exceptional regard for their environmental impact.

JOIST: Structural framing ELEMENTS running horizontally, supporting walls, roofs, and floors. Most often made of wood or metal.

LAMINATE: Paper fiber impregnated with melamine plastic to create a moisture-resistant sheet suitable for surfacing a SUBSTRATE vulnerable to water damage.

MANUFACTURED HOUSING: A house assembled on a steel frame that includes provisions for axles and wheels, making it possible to deliver the house to its site by towing it with a heavy truck.

MELAMINE: A hard, tough, glossy plastic with excellent resistance to moisture. Can be made in any desired color, and can be printed with designs.

MEMBRANE: A continuous "skin" that is impermeable to an undesirable condition, such as water or air intrusion. May be made of many different materials.

MOBILE HOME: An obsolete term for manufactured housing.

MODULAR HOUSING: A house made of large assemblies that can be transported on the bed of a truck, and then can be joined together to complete the structure.

NEWEL: A heavy post at the terminus of a stair's handrail, supporting the rail and its BALUSTERS.

ORGANIC ARCHITECTURE: A design philosophy derived from the teachings of Frank Lloyd Wright, who believed that "form follows function." Organic Architecture attempts to create forms that are visually related to their surroundings.

OSB: Oriented Strand Board. A wood-product material formed into sheets, composed of long, fibrous strands of wood compressed and adhered together. Not to be confused with PARTICLE BOARD, a material made of small particles of wood.

PANELIZED: Materials traditionally assembled by hand, combined into a mass-produced, modular ELEMENT that can be joined with like elements to produce wall, roof, and floor structures.

PARTICLE BOARD: An inexpensive wood-product material in sheet form, made of small particles of wood bound by an adhesive. Low in strength and moisture resistance; generally used only as a SUBSTRATE for more durable materials.

PEDESTAL FOUNDATION: A large, single-point support for a house, smaller than the house itself.

PIER: A small FOUNDATION element intended to support one point of a structure. Multiple piers are needed to support an entire house.

POLYCARBONATE: A high-strength plastic with excellent impact resistance and structural strength. Most familiar to consumers as the material used for food processor bowls, polycarbonate can be colored, or can be produced in a clear formulation difficult to distinguish visually from glass.

POLYESTER: A plastic resin that can be formed into components where durability and moisture resistance are required. Once extensively spun into yarns for clothing, polyester is frequently used today for kitchen and bath countertops.

POLYMER: A lightweight plastic that is easily molded into detailed shapes.

POLYSTYRENE: A plastic capable of being foamed; the air cells formed in the foam give polystyrene excellent insulating properties.

PRECAST: Formed into a usable ELEMENT in advance of installation by pouring or forcing a material into a mold; most often used to describe concrete ELEMENTS.

PREFAB: Prefabricated; assembled in advance of final installation, or consolidating several parts into one assembly.

P.S.I.: Pounds per Square Inch. A measure of the strength of materials like concrete, derived from how many pounds of pressure the material can withstand without damage.

R-VALUE: A numerical value that indicates how well a material resists heat loss. The higher the number, the greater the insulating property of the material.

RETAINING WALL: A wall intended to prevent ground movement on a site. Most often used to keep a slope from collapsing into a lower area at its base.

ROOF DECK: The part of a roof laid over its TRUSSES, forming continuous support for finish roofing.

SHOTCRETE: Concrete mix that can be sprayed from a gun onto a surface to form a continuous MEMBRANE of concrete.

SIP: Structural Insulated Panel. A wall or roof panel that consists of insulation sandwiched between outer layers, with internal support to give structural strength.

STUD: A vertical framing member within a wall; most often concealed by interior wall finish materials. Common stud materials for residential use are wood and steel. Long horizontal framing members are called JOISTS.

SUBSTRATE: A material used as a base for another material that serves as the surface of an object. Substrates are generally of more utilitarian materials than the surfaces applied to them. A kitchen counter is usually LAMINATE applied to a substrate of PARTICLE BOARD.

TRUSS: An assembly of ELEMENTS, often with a triangular form, intended to support heavy weights, such as roofs.

URETHANE: A rubbery synthetic often used for gaskets intended to seal windows against air leakage.

VINYL: A plastic that is lightweight and inexpensive, used to form ELEMENTS where structural strength is not essential. Highly resistant to moisture, fair impact resistance. Structural stiffness can be varied by adjustments to the plastic formula; vinyl can be quite rigid, or made into supple, flexible sheets.

Redi-Rock retaining wall.

Topsider home using a pedestal foundation system.

sources

A selection of companies and products mentioned in this book follows, categorized by housing system. The URLs given for company Web sites are current as of this book's publication but may change in the future. If in the future a Web site proves inaccessible, we recommend that you search for the company name using a search engine such as Google, putting the company name in quotes, as in "XYZ Manufacturing."

Many Web sites offer detailed product drawings in AutoCAD format. Look on the home page for links with such titles as "Drawings" or "For Architects." Generally, such drawings are free for download. Other information frequently offered includes copies of product warranties, but it's usually better to request a printed copy directly from the manufacturer, since information on Web sites is subject to change, and the warranty information online may not be current.

Many companies have toll-free numbers; these are often very helpful when product support is needed. Toll-free numbers are indicated, where applicable.

foundations & floor structures

KISTNER CONCRETE PRODUCTS, INC.
8713 Read Road
P.O. Box 218
East Pembroke, New York 14056
585-762-8216 telephone
www.kistner.com

The Thermal-Krete precast basement system utilizes panelized concrete walls to create dry, energy-efficient basements. Although primarily designed for new construction, the system can be applied to existing houses that have been temporarily removed from old or failing foundations.

MARINO\WARE
400 Metuchen Road
South Plainfield, New Jersey 07080
800-MARINO1 (627-4661) toll-free telephone
www.marinoware.com

The Joist-RITE steel framing system allows easy structural framing of floors and roofs. In addition to being fire-resistant, Joist-RITE's open spaces allow for easy passage of wiring and conduit Joist-RITE is designed for installation by experienced builders; owners should not expect to self-install this product.

PIN FOUNDATIONS, INC.
8607 58th Avenue, NW
Gig Harbor, Washington 98332
253-858-8809 telephone
www.pinfoundations.com

Patented, precast pier systems and wall-bearing systems, designed for low environmental impact, minimal ground disturbance, and ease of installation.

TOPSIDER HOMES
P.O. Box 1490
Clemmons, North Carolina 27012
866-867-9300 toll-free telephone
www.topsider.com

Prefabricated houses using post-and-beam construction, individually designed to owner specifications. A unique "pedestal foundation" system is available, raising the house above its terrain, and enabling installation on difficult building lots.

TREMCO BARRIER SOLUTIONS, INC.
6402 E. Main Street
Reynoldsburg, Ohio 43068
800-DRY-BSMT (379-2768) toll-free telephone
www.tuff-n-dri.com

The DrainStar Stripdrain basement drainage system replaces site-built, tile-and-gravel systems.

walls

BETTER BUILDING SYSTEMS, INC.
563 Idaho-Maryland Rd.
Grass Valley, California 95945
530-477-8017 telephone
www.betterbuilding.com

Custom structural insulated panels (SIPs) and complete housing packages; the company can produce panels to order for any house configuration needed. Its Nature House houses can be ordered in a wide variety of styles and configurations as shells whose interiors can be finished as desired.

HADRIAN TRIDI-SYSTEMS
909 W. Vista Way
Suite D
Vista, California 92083
888-682-2228 toll-free telephone
www.tridipanel.com

Steel, mesh-reinforced polystyrene building panels (SIPs), designed for a variety of exterior and interior finishes. When finished with shotcrete, Tridipanel forms a highly fire-resistant structure.

RAY-CORE, INC.
P.O. Box 66
Lock Haven, Pennsylvania 17745
570-748-6032 telephone
www.raycore.com

Polyurethane structural insulated panels (SIPs) for roofs and walls, incorporating a shiplap joint at their edges to promote watertight installation. Ray-Core panels weigh only 43 pounds each, are formaldehyde free, and include wood studs in each panel.

REDI-ROCK INTERNATIONAL, LLC
05481 US 31 South
Charlevoix, MI 49720
866-222-8400 toll-free telephone
www.redi-rock.com

Precast, interlocking retaining wall elements, as well as interlocking elements to create freestanding fencing walls.

THERMAPAN STRUCTURAL INSULATED PANELS
1380 Commerce Parkway
Fort Erie, Ontario
L2A 5M4
Canada
905-994-7399 telephone
www.thermapan.com

Thermapan SIPs are polyurethane-core, wood-faced panels with excellent insulating qualities; they have been used successfully in Arctic conditions.

glazing

SOLATUBE INTERNATIONAL, INC.
2210 Oak Ridge Way
Vista, California 92081
800-966-7652 toll-free telephone
www.solatube.com

Skylights that require no framing, and accessories increasing their versatility, such as motorized shutters to block light when desired.

SOLAR INNOVATIONS, INC.
234 East Rosebud Road
Myerstown, Pennsylvania 17067
800-618-0669 toll-free telephone
www.solarinnovations.com

Solariums, glass curtain walls, greenhouses, skylights, conservatories, walkways, canopies, and pool enclosures, in both contemporary and traditional styles.

Solatube International skylight.

Focal Point molded architectural elements.

interior elements

ADAMS STAIR, INC.
1083 South Corporate Circle
Grayslake, Illinois 60030
847-223-1177 telephone
www.adamsstair.com

Prefabricated stair units in a wide
variety of contemporary and traditional
styles. Units can be shipped
unassembled or ready to install. Extensive
customization is available.

FOCAL POINT, INC.
3006 Anaconda Drive
Tarboro, North Carolina 27886
800-662-5550 toll-free telephone
www.focalpointap.com

Molded architectural interior elements,
including domes, moldings, and
columns in both traditional and some
contemporary designs. Focal Point is
authorized by several major historic
societies, such as the Colonial Williamsburg
Foundation and The Frank Lloyd Wright
Foundation, to offer reproductions of
important historic molding profiles and
other elements.

GLOBAL STONE COMPANY
3120 46th Avenue North
St. Petersburg, Florida 33714
727-521-0094 telephone
www.globalstone.net

Prefabricated marble and stone kitchen and
bath counters; installation accessories and
products are available.

HOMASOTE COMPANY
P.O. Box 7240
932 Lower Ferry Road
West Trenton, New Jersey 08628
800-257-9491 toll-free telephone
www.homasote.com

Wall panels manufactured from post-
consumer recycled paper, with several
surface finishes, including fabric. A sound-
absorbing panel product is also available;
Homasote products can be ordered in
several fire ratings.

roofs

DURO-LAST ROOFING, INC.
525 Morley Drive
Saginaw, Michigan 48601
800-248-0280 toll-free telephone
www.duro-last.com

Thermoplastic, netting-reinforced single-ply
roofing membrane especially suited to low-
slope and flat roofs. Easily repaired; requires
professional installation through
Duro-Last's network of affiliate installers.

**ONDURA CORRUGATED ROOFING DIVISION,
TALLANT INDUSTRIES, INC.**
4994 Ondura Drive
Fredericksburg, Virginia 22407
800-777-7663 toll-free telephone
www.ondura.com

Asphalt-impregnated, corrugated roofing in a
wide variety of colors; extremely well suited
for DIY installation. Ondura is also available in
a design that resembles Spanish tile when
installed. The installation can be completed
with Ridgeline ridge venting. Tuftex clear
corrugated panels can be used for
transparent roofing and walls.

additions / freestanding structures

FAZE CHANGE PRODUX
R.R. #1
P.O. Box 295B
Sullivan, Illinois 61951
888-DOMELUV (366-3588) toll-free telephone
www.one-eleven.net/~econodome

Manufacturers of Econ-O-Dome geodesic
dome kits. The domes are usable as
freestanding additions; Faze Change
produces a freestanding garage as well.

MODULAR DWELLINGS
2729 Acton Street
Berkeley, California 94702
415-350-4904 telephone
www.modulardwellings.com

Modernist freestanding structures in sizes up
to 420 square feet, suitable for use as
guesthouses, offices, media rooms, and for
other purposes. Larger versions
incorporating kitchens and baths are
planned. Modular Dwellings use Pin
Foundation's Diamond Pier footing system as
their foundations.

OSKAR LEO KAUFMANN
Steinebach 3
6850 Dornbirn
Austria
43-5572-39-49-69 telephone
www.olk.cc

Architect Kaufmann is responsible for the
OA.SYS system of prefabricated panels that
can be combined in different ways to produce
various structures. His SU-SI prefabricated
house is a complete, packaged house that
can be trucked to site and installed quickly.

credits

Courtesy Focal Point Architectural Products, Inc., pp. 1, 88, 89, 90, 91, 117, 136, 140

Paul Bardagjy, pp. 2–3, 33, 34, 35

Courtesy Redi-Rock International, pp. 4–5, 50 (right), 51, 69, 70, 71, 122 (right), 130–131

Courtesy Oskar Leo Kaufmann, pp. 6–7, 51 (right), 103, 104, 105, 106, 107

Tim Street-Porter/Esto, pp. 9, 10–11

Photograph of Fallingwater Courtesy Western Pennsylvania Conservancy. Fallingwater is located in Mill Run, Pennsylvania, Telephone: 724-329-8501, pp. 23

Royalty-Free/Corbis, pp. 15 (left), 17, 37

Photo by Ernest Braun/Courtesy Eichler Network Archives, pp. 19, 29

Richard A. Cooke/Corbis, pp. 14 (left), 20

Farrell Graham/Corbis, pp. 22–23

Ezra Stoller/Esto, pp. 25

Jon Miller/Hedrich Blessing, pp. 14 (right), 26–27

Bettmann/Corbis, pp. 30

Courtesy Dupont Surfaces, pp. 38–39 (Zodiaq®), 51 (right), 92–93 (Zodiaq®), 94, 95 (Zodiaq®), 139, 144. More information is available at www.corian.com or by calling 800-4-CORIAN. More information is available at www.zodiaq.com or by calling toll-free 877-229-3935.

Robert Reck Photography/Courtesy Bart Prince, pp. 40–41, 42–43, 44–45

Courtesy Patrick Seabol, pp. 15 (right), 46, 47, 48, 49

Courtesy Topsider Homes, pp. 53, 59, 82, 125, 132–133

Courtesy Pin Foundations, Inc., pp. 56, 114 (left), 123 (left)

Courtesy Edgar Blazona, pp. 57, 108, 109, 110, 111, 122 (left)

Courtesy Better Building Systems, Inc., pp. 63, 123 (right)

Courtesy Insulspan, Inc., pp. 64, 65, 114 (right)

Courtesy Hadrian Tridi Systems, pp. 66, 67

John Dunn/Articlight, pp. 73

Rodney Hyett/Elizabeth Whiting & Associates/Corbis, pp. 75, 83, 96, 97

Elizabeth Whiting & Associates/Corbis, pp. 50 (right), 76

Courtesy Solatube International, pp. 77, 78, 115 (left), 135

Courtesy Solar Innovations, Inc., pp. 80

Courtesy Adams Stair, pp. 84, 85, 86, 87

Courtesy Duro-Last Roofing, Inc., pp. 99

Courtesy Tallant Industries, pp. 100, 115 (right)

Mark E. Gibson/Corbis, pp. 113

Corian countertop for kitchens.

index

A

Adams Stair Company, *84–87,* 85, 137
Adobe Acrobat Reader, 118
Archie Teater Studio (Bliss, Idaho), 24
architects, 124
AutoCAD drawings, 116, 118, 124,
    126–27, 133
Autodesk DWF Composer, 118, 126
Autodesk DWF Viewer, 118, 126

B

bathrooms, 16, *16–17,* 32, *35,* 36,
    82–83, 93
Better Building Systems, 62–63, 134
Blazona, Edgar, *56–57,* 58, 107, *108–11,*
    111
Brighten Up skylights, 77
building codes, 120–21, 124

C

CAD (Computer-Assisted Design), 82, 85
CAD software, 118–19, 124, 126–27
CADopia IntelliCAD 4 Professional Edition,
    127
CADopia IntelliCAD Flamingo, 127
CADopia IntelliCAD Rhino, 127
CADopia IntelliCAD Standard Edition 4, 127
CADVANCE, 127
California Modern, 28
canopies, 134

Case Study Houses, 8, *9–11,* 11, 28
ceramic tile, 82
closed-cell polymer, 88, 93
CNC (Computer Numerically Controlled), 82, 85
cold climates, 72
Colonial Williamsburg Foundation, 93, 137
conservatories, 74, *74–76, 80–81,* 134
Contour-All, 88, 93
Contractor-Books.com, 120
Corian, 13, 39, 93, *94–95, 138–39*
countertops, 13, *24–25,* 31, 36, 39,
    92–97, 93, 137, *138–39*
"Country Clubber" model, 31
Crystal Palace (London), 81

D

Daylight Dimmer, 77
DesignWall, 96
Diamond Piers, *56–57,* 57–58, 107,
    108–9, 137
dimension control, 18
do-it-yourself market, 116
doors, 18, 36, *48–49*
    bifold, 31
    panels on, 32
    replacement, 47
    sliding, 31, 32
drainage, 60
DrainStar Stripdrain system, 60–61, 133
Duro-Last Roofing, 98–99, *98–99,* 101, 137
DWF file format, 119, 124, 126–27
DWG file format, 119

E

Eames, Charles and Ray, 8, 11, 28, 111
Eames House (Case Study House #8), 8,
    9–11, 11
Econ-O-Dome, 112, 137
Eichler, Joseph, 28, *28–29,* 31, 99
Eichler houses, *18–19,* 99, 101
elastomeric paint finish, 112, *112–13*
energy efficiency, 74

F

Fallingwater (Pennsylvania), *20–23,* 21
Farnsworth House, 24, *26–27,* 28
Faze Change Produx, 112, 137
Fidroeff, Wil, 112
fire resistance, 56, 66–67
fireplaces, 31, *48–49*
F.I.T. CADVANCE 6.5, 127
floor structures, 54–58, 60–61, 133
flooring, 36, *36–37*
Focal Point Architectural Products, 88,
    88–91, 93, *116–17,* 137, *140*
FocalFlex, 88, 93
Ford House, 43
Formica, 13, 18, *24–25*
foundations, 40, 47, 54–58, 60–61,
    108–9, 132, 133
440 SoundBarrier, 96–97
Frank Lloyd Wright Collection, 93, 137
FRED room units, *106–7,* 107
Fuller, Buckminster, 112, *112*

Focal Point molded architectural elements.

G

Gamble, Brice, 111
General Electric, 32, *32–33*
geo-grid, 72
geodesic domes, 112, *112–13*, 137
Gillen Manufacturing Company, 21, 24
glazing, 52, 74, *75–76*, 77, *78–80*, 81,
    134. *See also* windows
Global Stone Company, 93, 137
Goff, Bruce, 40, 43
Gradow Residence, *40–43*, 43–44, 58
greenhouses, *80–81*, 134

H

Habitat for Humanity houses, 72
Hadrian, Ron, 66
Hadrian Tridi-Systems, 66–67, *66–67*, 134
Homasote, 96–97, 137
Home Again, 116
"Hoosier" units, 21
Hope's, 21

I

injection-molded plastics, 36
installation, 119–20
insulation, 54, 55, 66, 67–68, 96
interiors, *6–7*, 82, *82–97*, 85, 88, 93,
    96–97, *136*, 137
International Style, 24, 28, 32
Internet, research on, 116, 118

J

Joist-RITE floor joists, 55–57, 133
Jones House (Tulsa), 21

K

Kaufmann, Oskar Leo, *6–7*, 102, *104–7*,
    107, 137
Kesling Modern Homes, 28
Kesling, William, 28
KeyCAD PRO, 127
Kistner Concrete Products, Inc., 54–55, 133
kitchen cabinetry, 21, *23*, 24, *24–25*,
    34–35, *48–49*, 82, *82*
   metal, 28, *30–31*, 31
   wood, 31, 36, *38–39*
Koenig, Pierre, 28, 39

L

laminate flooring, 36, *36–37*
lauan plywood, *18–19*
Levitt, William J., 28
Levittown, 28, 31
linen units, 24
LITD (Light Intercepting Transfer Device), 77

M

manufacturer-authorized installers, 120
manufacturer-recommended installers,
    119–20
Marino\WARE, 55–57, 133
metal flashing, 101
Mies van der Rohe, Ludwig, 24, *26–27*,
    28, 39
Modular Dwellings, 107, *108–11*, 111, 137
modular post-and-beam construction, *18–19*
moldings, 88, *88–91*, 137

N

Nature House designs, 63, 66, 134
Neutra, Richard, 39, 111

O

OA.SYS, *6–7*, 102, *102–5*, 107, 137
Ondura roofing sheets, *100–101*, 101, 137
Open Architecture System, 102, 107
oriented strand board (OSB), 62–63
owner-selected professional installers, 119

P

Palm Springs houses, *46–49*
Parsifal Townhomes, 44, *44–45*, 47
patios, *4–5*
PDF (portable document file), 118
pedestal foundations, 58, *58–61*, 60,
    132, 133
Pella Glass, 24
Pergo, 36
Pin Foundations, Inc., 57–58, 107, 133,
    137
Pittsburgh Plate Glass, 24
"pod" formations, 43–44
PolyCarbonate, 101
polyester resin, 16
polystyrene insulation, 66
ponding, 98
pool enclosures, *80–81*, 134
Pope-Leighey House, 81
prefab elements. *See also specific elements*
   advantages of, 16, 18, *97*
   building codes and, 120–21, 124
   flexibility and variety of, 13
   history of, 8, 11, 18, 21, 24, 28,
      31–32, 36, 39–40, 43–44, 47
   for older houses, 47
   planning for, 52
   price and, 12–13, 16, 47, *48–49*
   researching, 116, 118–20
Prince, Bart, 40, *40–45*, 43–44, 47, 58
purlins, 101

Q

Quonset huts, 43

R

Ray-Core, Inc., 67–68, 134
Raybender Fresnel lens, 77
Redi-Rock Inc., *4–5*, 68, *68–71*, 72,
        130–31, 134
ridge ventilation, 101
Ridgeline, 101, 137
roof panels, 62, 68
roof trusses, *64–65*
roofs, 40, 47, 98–99, 101, 137
room additions and freestanding structures,
        102, *102–11*, 107, 111–12, 137

S

safety, 18
St. Charles Kitchens, 21, *23*
"saturated seal," 112
Seabol, Patrick, *46–49*
sealing gaskets, 74, 77
Sheetrock, 62, 96, 112
shingles, 98
shiplap joint, 68
shotcrete, 66–67, *66–67*
showers, 16, 39, 82, *82–83*
skylights, 74, 77, 134, *134–35*
snow loads, 72, 112
Solar Innovations, Inc., *74–75*, 77, 81, 134
solariums, 134
Solatube, 77, *78–79*, 134, *134–35*
sound control, 96–97, 102
stairs, *84–87*, 85, 137
steel joists, 55–57
storage cabinets, 16, 21, 24
structural insulated panels (SIPs), 62–63,
        62–67, 67–68, 98, 134

"Style in Steel Townhouses," 32, *32–35*
SU-SI prefab house, 137
sunrooms, 74, 101
synthetics, 36

T

Tallant Industries, 101, 137
tar, 98
Thermal-Krete system, 54–55, 133
Thermapan SIPs, 72, *72–73*, 134
This Old House, 116
Topsider Homes, 58, *58–59*, 60, *125*,
        132, 133
Tremco Barrier Solutions, Inc., 60–61, 133
Tridipanels, 66–67, *66–67*, 134
tubs, 16, 39, 82
TUFF-N-DRI, 61
Tuftex, 101, 137

U

urethane gaskets, 74, 81
Usonian houses, 24, *24–25*
UV filtering, 77

V

vanities, 16, 82–83
Vila, Bob, 116
vinyl flooring, 36
vinyl siding, 36

W

Walker House (Carmel), 24
walkways, 134

walls, *18–19*, 62–63, *63–67*, 66–68,
        69–71, 72, *73*, *130–31*, 134
    glass, 32, 40, 74, *80–81*, 81, 134
    interior, 32
warranties, 119–20
WATCHDOG WATERPROOFING, 61
waterproofing, 40, 55, 61
Weatherford, Hal, 32
weatherproofing, 112
Web sites, company, 116, 118, 126, 133
Wilson, Talbott, 32
Wilson Morris Crain and Anderson
        Architects, 32
window walls, 32, *80–81*
windows, *16–17*, 18, 36, *48–49*, 74,
        104–5
    aluminum-framed, 31
    mullions on, 32
    replacement, 47
    steel units, 21, *22–23*, 28
"wood-grain" vinyl, 32
wooden floor joists, 55
Wright, Frank Lloyd, *20–23*, 21, 24, *24–25*,
        39, 40, 81

Z

Zolatone, *28–29*